Ten Requirements for America's Survival

Dr. David O. Dykes

Ten Requirements for America's Survival
by Dr. David O. Dykes

Printed in the United States of America

ISBN 1-594677-90-5

For a complete list of books and broadcast messages by Dr. David O. Dykes available in print, CD/Cassette or VHS/DVD, please visit the Discover Life online Resource Center at www.discoverlife.tv. Order 24 hours a day.

> Green Acres Baptist Church
> 1607 Troup Highway
> Tyler, Texas 75701
> www.gabc.org

Produced with the assistance of Fluency in Tyler, Texas.

www.xulonpress.com

Table of Contents

INTRODUCTION

Will America Survive in the 21st Century?

In the sultry summer heat of 2003, one man's passionate pursuit of his convictions headlined the front pages of newspapers across our nation. Alabama Chief Justice Roy Moore gave a statement of noncompliance regarding an order by a Federal court judge ordering Moore to remove the stone depiction of the Ten Commandments from the rotunda of the Alabama Judicial Building. In doing so, Moore thrust religious liberty onto the national scene once again. This wasn't the first time these ten phrases etched in stone had been the focal point of intense arguments on the network news or had sparked ardent conversations at the local diner. On one side, proponents say it's about the right to recognize God publicly in our nation, while opponents vehemently point to the separation of church and state.

Since when did ten phrases, concise enough to fit on one-half page, garner so much attention and result in so much misunderstanding? When did truth go up for grabs and become relegated to societal platitudes like, "If it feels good, do it"? After all, the Ten Commandments have stood as the world's most succinct standard to distinguish between truth and error for over 30 centuries. Despite the liberal media's insistence to the contrary, our nation's Founding Fathers never intended for the so-called "wall of separation" between church and state to protect the government from Christian influence. They designed it to protect the *church* from governmental interference.

There is no question that throughout the majority of America's history, both state and federal governments have translated the principles of the Ten Commandments into laws (e.g., prohibitions against murder and theft). Although many laws (against adultery and Sunday business closings, etc.,) have been nullified in recent years, Judge Moore's case is of even greater significance. It is the first time a state official, and therefore the state, has been prohibited from publicly recognizing God. Despite the fact that Moore was in direct compliance with the preamble of the Alabama and US Constitution, both of which reference God, and despite the three depictions of the Ten Commandments and Moses displayed in the Supreme Court building to this day, Moore was charged with an ethics violation and summarily removed from office in November 2003.

Ironically, many well-intentioned Christian advisors counseled Judge Moore to reconsider his unyielding strategy, suggesting that he placate his opponents and downplay the religious significance of the Commandments. In so doing, perhaps Moore could have kept his job and the monument would remain to this day. However, I greatly admire Judge Moore's stalwart commitment to what he knew was right—even if it meant losing his livelihood and risking public humiliation. If America is going to survive into the 21st century, an army of Christians with the same fervor and commitment to truth as Judge Moore demonstrated will have to arise against the tide of popular opinion. If we do not stand up for the moral and religious roots of the freedoms we enjoy as Americans, judicial tyranny will continue to whittle away at our country's historically biblical foundations. It's not difficult to see how this could pave the way for the eventual persecution of Bible-believing Christians on an unprecedented national scale.

Those who sincerely believe the Ten Commandments represent the entire basis of our system of government can see how much is at stake today. When we weaken our resolve to the godly and moral principles our Founding Fathers and our heavenly Father gave us, we weaken the very foundation upon which this great nation is built. Which makes the question that much more significant, "Will America survive into the 21st century?" In large part, it's up to you.

CHAPTER 1

Who Is America's God?

"And God spoke all these words: I am the Lord your God, who brought you out of Egypt, out of the land of slavery. You shall have no other gods before me."
Exodus 20:1

B efore Monica, Ken Starr or a number of other internationally embarrassing Clinton-era scandals including Travelgate, there was Watergate. In 1974, President Nixon was forced to resign because of the ensuing heat from the Watergate Investigation stemming from a break-in at the Democratic National Committee's headquarters. One of the key characters in the Watergate scenario, Presidential advisor Jeb McGruder, was convicted of burglary and cover-up. Upon sentencing McGruder, an incredulous Judge Siricca asked him, "How could it happen? How could you fall such as you did?"

McGruder morosely replied, "Somewhere along the way, I lost my moral compass and with it, the ability to navigate my life." For many Americans, wandering around in an ethical fog, confusion about what is right and what is wrong has set in because they too have lost their moral compass.

However, God is not subject to the "spin" swirling around the issues. He has an absolute standard of truth - right and wrong -

black and white. If America hopes to survive far into the 21st century, we must reinstate the basic standards of morality represented in the Ten Commandments. They are not polite options; they are ABSOLUTE REQUIREMENTS for America's survival.

Ted Koppel, longtime anchor for ABC Evening News, once said, "Our society finds truth too strong a medicine to digest undiluted. In its purest form, truth is not a polite tap on the shoulder; it's a howling reproach. When Moses walked down from Mt. Sinai, he brought the Ten Commandments, not the Ten Suggestions." [i] Our only hope for survival is to admit that God has not changed His moral standards - we have simply ignored them. American Christians must hear and obey the voice of God when He said, "If my people, who are called by my name, will humble themselves and pray and seek my face and turn from their wicked ways, then will I hear from heaven and will forgive their sin and will heal their land" (2 Chronicles 7:14).

Every dollar and every coin at the U.S. Mint has the words, *In God We Trust*, boldly printed at the top. But who is America's God? And how has America's understanding changed regarding who God is and what He requires? In answer to those questions, we'd have to go back in our minds 33 centuries, long before our relatively short history as a nation, and witness an amazing scene in the desert on the Sinai Peninsula in the Middle East. Historians estimate from 250,000 to 2 million Hebrew people were gathered on that plain on their journey from the slavery of Egypt to the freedom of Canaan. From the desert floor, the Sinai Mountains rise about 4500 feet above sea level. Above that range of mountains is the soaring, altar-shaped Mount Sinai itself. Mt. Sinai stands above the other mountains as if it is lifting its face to God. This is the place where God assembled the Children of Israel to reveal who He is (His character) and what He expects (His laws) for all generations. He did this in the form of the Ten Commandments—a thunderous event accompanied by fire, clouds and lightning that announced God's presence (Exodus 19).

Two of the most pressing questions of life are DOES GOD EXIST and WHAT IS HE LIKE? However, immediately after considering that, we must ask, WHAT DOES GOD EXPECT OF

ME? God's first requirement is that we have no gods other than Himself. In this first requirement, God reveals something to us about who He is. God's first revelation is His name, *"I am the Lord."*

Who Is God?

In gatherings where there are people I do not know, I always appreciate it when someone provides nametags that say, "Hello. My name is _____." That makes me feel more comfortable in a new environment. Once we know someone's name, we are on the way to knowing something about him or her. That is exactly what God was doing. It's as if He put on a nametag that said, "Hello. My name is Yahweh."

The original Hebrew language spelled God's name with these four consonants, **Y H W H.** There are no vowels in the original Hebrew, only 22 consonants. Even though modern Hebrew has added vowel points to aid in pronunciation, translators have had to guess what the vowel sounds were like. These four consonants, Y H W H (called the "Tetragrammaton"), appear more than 6,000 times in the Old Testament.

Anyone who has studied biblical Hebrew knows it is a challenging language and is often hard to decipher. Let me give you an idea of how Hebrew is often hard to read—even for the most educated. One of my seminary colleagues took his Hebrew Bible to the library to work on translating. He had been attempting to translate his work for about 15 frustrating minutes when a graduate student walked by and commented that my friend was holding his Hebrew Bible upside down! Someone has observed that ancient Hebrew looks like a couple of chickens have dipped their feet in ink and walked across a paper! This is why we are exactly unsure about the pronunciation of YHWH, although the most agreed upon pronunciation is YAH-WAY.

However, the Hebrew people never spoke the name of God. The name was so holy they would never speak it aloud because they were afraid they might pronounce it incorrectly, which would constitute blasphemy. Since they refused to pronounce YHWH, they would always substitute another Hebrew word, ***adonai***, which means "Lord." Anytime we see the English word "Lord," in the Old Testament it is actually YHWH.

You may be wondering at this point, "Where did we get the word *Jehovah* (another name for God)?" The Latin Vulgate was the first translation of the Bible into another language, and the German language was the second. In German, the "Y" is a "J," and a "W" is a "V" sound, so the Germanized translation of YAHWEH is JEHO-VAH. God's German name is *Jehovah*, but His Hebrew name is *Yahweh*. If someone comes to you insisting that you must call God "Jehovah," you can now set him or her straight. God "goes" by both!

God Has Always Been

Another interesting aspect of the Hebrew language is that it doesn't share our concept of tense. In English, we have past, present and future tense. In Hebrew, when God said, "I am Yahweh," He wasn't limiting Himself to time and space. He was saying, "I've always been, I am right now, and I'll always be." The best way to translate that is, *"I am being itself; I am Yahweh."* There has never been a time when God was not "being." The word "Yahweh" means He is the Creator who has always existed.

The Bible never tries to prove the existence of God. Sometimes, people try to find a verse of Scripture that proves the existence of God. You won't find one. The Bible begins with the assumption there is a God and He is the Creator. Genesis 1:1 begins, *"In the beginning God created. . ."* Sometimes people try to find God or prove the existence of God by over-analyzing the Bible. You cannot take your Bible apart to find the existence of God any easier than you could take a piano apart to try to find music. Music is *in* the piano, and it comes out through the one who plays it. God is in the Bible, and God is in this world when we just know how and where to find Him.

God Is a Big God

Because God has always been, He alone is the Creator of all there is. The name "Yahweh" can best be rendered "organizer, creator, ruler, the one who reigns." You may be familiar with the little chorus entitled, "Our God Reigns." I heard about one church that had a misspelling in its Sunday bulletin. Instead of saying, "Our God Reigns" a typist mistakenly added an extra "s" and it read, "Our God Resigns." God HASN'T resigned, He rules! He is in charge because He is the Creator of everything.

In spite of many theories about how our universe began, I have no problem believing God simply spoke the universe into existence. When we understand how massive the universe is, we stand in awe at the greatness and majesty of God. It is a humbling experience for us to realize that we are only a minuscule dot in an enormous universe.

To reduce outer space into terms you can grasp, just imagine that our sun is the size of a pinhead and our own solar system is revolving around this pinhead-sized sun. If you put the sun (the pinhead) in the center and our solar system around it, it would fill up a 12 x 12 room. In that scenario, the earth is nothing but a tiny speck of dust. It's called "outer space," because it is mostly space. Now, that is just our solar system. It fits inside the den of your home.

Using that same scale, if you wanted to go to the next nearest star in our galaxy (another pinhead), you would have to go 26 miles down the road to find it. Astronomers tell us that our galaxy, the Milky Way, is only one of at least 400 million galaxies. Using this same scale, you would have to travel 300,000 miles to get to the next galaxy!

In Psalm 8, the Psalmist stands in awe and writes, *"When I consider the heavens, the work of your fingers. . ."* God did it—with just His fingers! I wonder how anyone could look at life or look at the universe and doubt there is an intelligent Designer and Creator behind it all.

God Is into Details

Another way to consider the greatness of God is to examine your own bodies. Your body is comprised of millions of individual cells. Dr. Paul Dody, a microbiologist at John Hopkins University, has said that each individual cell of our body is more complex and intricate than New York City. A single cell! Each of your cells has a more detailed infrastructure than the busiest city in America. When you observe the macrocosm of the universe or the microcosm of a human body, you have to acknowledge that there is an intelligent creator. Just now as I'm writing this, I'm looking at my wristwatch. When I examine it, I can't deny the reality that somebody designed it and manufactured it. It has the name "Zodiac" stamped on the face. My watch did not just happen as the result of an explosion of a bunch of little metal parts. If I claimed that my watch "just happened" by some kind of random fortuitous concurrence of glass and metal, others would scoff at me. Yet otherwise intelligent people say that our universe came into existence the same way.

In the late 90s, people were excited by news reports about the possible discovery of ancient life on planet Mars. Some scientists acted as if that were the greatest discovery ever made, but I disagreed. I have always contended that the greatest discovery in this universe is not that other life exists but that **God exists**. Can you think of anything that would be more life changing than that one fact? The second greatest fact is: **you can know Him**. This is a personal discovery that each person must make. It is not hidden; this truth has been available for over 3,000 years.

In 1492, Columbus sailed westward from Europe looking for India. When he got to the Caribbean he named the islands the West Indies, and he called the people he found "Indians." He returned to Spain and declared, "I have discovered a new world." Columbus didn't invent it or create it because it had been there all along. He just stumbled on to it. Some people believed him, but many would not believe until they saw for themselves—so others traveled to this new world.

The same is true with knowing God. We do not invent that relationship; it has been a possibility since God revealed Himself at Sinai. However, each of us must make this personal discovery for ourselves. God will not force you to have fellowship with Him, but He loves you and He desires to have a relationship with you.

God Is Seeking You

God is shaping our circumstances to draw us to Himself. In Exodus 20:2, He says, *"I am the Lord your God, who brought you out of Egypt, out of the land of slavery."* God is saying, "Children of Israel, I've been shaping the circumstances of your life, to bring you to the point where I can open up to you and reveal Myself to you." I believe God is saying the same thing to us today. He is saying, "I've brought you to this point in your life so that you can know Me, so that I can be all that you need in life. You didn't arrive here by accident; your presence here is not incidental; it is intentional."

In hindsight, we can look behind us to see all the things God has done to shape our circumstances to bring us to the point where He can conform us to the image of His Son, Jesus Christ (Romans 8:29). He says, "Not only do I seek your fellowship, I'll shape your circumstances so that you can know Me."

Psalm 53:1 says this, *"The fool says in his heart, `There is no God.'"* Sometimes we mistakenly think the word 'fool' means someone who is intellectually deficient. The word is <u>nabal</u> in Hebrew. According to God's standards, a <u>nabal</u> is someone who is morally deficient and chooses to live an immoral, empty life.

The fool doesn't say, "I have intellectual hang-ups about the possibility of God, therefore He doesn't exist." According to this verse, the fool is actually saying, "I don't **want** any God. No God for me, thank you."

After you have eaten a delicious meal, your host may say, "Would you like some dessert?" Sometimes you are so full you respond, "No dessert." You are not denying the reality of that dessert, you aren't even denying that dessert tastes good, you are just saying, "No dessert for me."

The Bible says a fool is confronted with God's offer and says, "No God for me." God's offer is available to everyone, but He gives us a choice about accepting His offer. That is the most profound discovery you will ever make—that God exists, that He loves you and wants to know you.

No Rivals Allowed
The final lesson we learn from the first commandment is the primary demand from God. God has said, "This is who I am. This is what I have done. This is what I require of you." Then He says in Exodus 20:3, *"You will have no other gods before me."* When you read that, you may think He is referring to some of those obscure pagan gods of that time like Dagon, Baal, Zeus or Mercury. You may think you are safe because you don't worship those ancient

gods. If you think idolatry is only about bowing down to a totem pole or some statue of a god, you are mistaken.

A god is anything or anybody that orders our lives. For some people, their job is their god because their job receives the majority of their attention and effort. For others, a hobby has become their god, because it is what drives their life. And some have even made their family their god. God loves our families and wants our families to love Him, but it's possible to substitute something as noble as a family for the living God. Gods can include hobbies, money, success, power, and the list can go on and on.

To find your "god," you can apply the "T" test. As yourself:

What do I **THINK** about most?

What do I **TALK** about most?

Where do I invest my **TREASURE**?

Where do I spend all my **TIME**?

When you can identify what you talk about, think about, where you invest your time and treasure, you have identified your god. If it is not Yahweh, the God of the Bible, you are violating this first requirement. God says, "I won't tolerate any rival gods. This is my primary demand."

Since the command, "No other gods before me" is placed in the negative, how can you understand that command from a positive perspective? First, you ought to seek God earnestly, sincerely, and seek to let God be your only God. In Jeremiah 29:13, God says, *"You will seek me and you will find me when you seek for me with your whole heart."* Some people seek God halfheartedly, passively, with a "take it or leave it" attitude. If you show up for church occasionally and only pray and read the Word of God sporadically, then you aren't really seeking God earnestly.

Through the years, I have played a number of musical instruments. I have played the guitar since I was in the eighth grade, and I also play (a little) the string base, mandolin and banjo. Several years ago, I picked up a violin, hoping to add it to my repertoire. *How hard can it be?* I remember thinking to myself. My playing sounded like two cats in one bag. It was awful. After two or three more unsuccessful attempts at mastering the violin, I finally decided there is just no music in a violin. Of course, I was wrong.

Accomplished violinists who have invested years of diligent practice to master that instrument could play music on one string of an old violin and bring tears to our eyes. What is the difference? These violinists have applied themselves to the violin. They have sought expertise with a single-minded diligence. That is the key to a dynamic relationship with God as well.

If you don't apply yourselves and earnestly seek after God, you might be tempted to think that this relationship "doesn't work." You might feel that there are no blessings, joy or peace from God. In order to experience these blessings, you must seek God exclusively. There is room for only one God in your life.

Only One Number One

Who is number one for you? Numbers are amazing entities. The number one is a number different from any other number. For example, a man who has one wife is in a very different category from a man who has two, three, five, twenty, thirty or, like Solomon, a thousand wives. The difference between one and two is a giant leap compared to the step between two and two million. It is not a difference in degree; it is a difference in type. A man with only one wife is a monogamist, and a man who has two or twenty wives is called a polygamist.

A student in sociology class forgot the correct word for this fill-in-the-blank quiz question: "A man who has only one wife is practicing _____." The correct answer was "monogamy," but she accidentally wrote the word "monotony." Actually, marriage as God intended it to be is NEVER monotonous! Think about this is relation to God. It doesn't matter if you have two gods or a thousand gods. Having only ONE God is a fundamental difference.

Being from Texas, I like the Dallas Cowboys. I admire the former Cowboy star, Emmett Smith. In 1996, an article in *Sports Illustrated* featured Emmett sharing his list of priorities for the year. Emmett said his top priority was to keep Jesus Christ number one in his life. Number two was to win another Super Bowl. Number three was to stay healthy. Number four was to win the rushing title again. Number five, to be named to the Pro Bowl.

When I read something like that, my initial reaction is "Wow!

That's great. I'm glad Emmett loves the Lord and wants Jesus number one." However, when you look below the surface there is a real danger is this attitude. God refuses to be number one on a list of several things. Why? Even if we place God first on a list of many things, we degrade God by comparing Him to any of those other things. God declines to be number one on a list of three things. God won't accept being number one on a list of even two things. God insists, He demands, that **He be number one on a list of one**.

Some people misunderstand what this commandment is all about. They think that when God says to "have no other gods before me," it means to keep Him number one and not to put anything on the list before Him. However, that is not what it means. What God is saying is, "I won't tolerate any other gods in My presence. I don't want to be One of many. I want to be THE One."

My wife and I have been happily married for over 25 years. If I told Cindy, "You're my number one wife—there's number two, three, four—but, you are number one," she would not be very happy! She doesn't want to be my number one wife on a list of three or four. God is the same way. He demands that we seek Him exclusively. That is what the first commandment is all about.

Who is number one for you? Where are you putting your time? Your treasure? Your thoughts? What do you talk about the most? The answers show who is number one or you, no matter how religiously you may "talk." At your greatest time of need, false gods will never come through for you; they will fail you every time. In your time of need, the only One who will ever come through for you is the Lord God Jehovah, Yahweh, the God Who has always been, Who is and Who will always be. How can you know Him? How can you seek Him? The New Testament tells us how—through Jesus Christ. He is the exclusive connection to God the Father.

It Is Finished

In the last century, railroads were the primary mode of transportation. Many railroads crossed the eastern part of the country, but because of the Rocky Mountains, no network of railroads traversed the western part of our nation until the Central Pacific and Union Pacific Railroad companies started an optimistic project called the

Transcontinental Railroad. They started in St. Louis, Missouri, building a railroad westward, and they started in San Francisco, California, building a railroad eastward through the Rocky Mountains. On May 10, 1869, outside of Ogden, Utah, the two teams finally met. You may have seen photographs of this encounter, where two train engines, workers, dignitaries and a band gathered to mark the occasion. When the railroad workers laid the last rail, they took a ceremonial golden spike and a silver hammer and pounded that golden spike into that last rail.

When they finally drove in that final golden spike, the conductors blew their train whistles, people threw their hats into the air, the band began to play and the railroad dignitaries shouted, "Finally! East and West are joined together by a single track! It's finished!"

This picture makes me think about what Jesus did for us when He laid an arm on each side of the cross. The Roman soldiers did not have a golden spike; they took a rusty spike. It was not a silver hammer they used to pin his flesh to the cross; it was an iron hammer. And they pounded that spike into the quivering flesh of the Son of God. Why was Jesus on the cross? Fully God (sinless, pure and holy) and fully man, he reached out to sinful, fallen, depraved humanity. When Jesus took the hand of a holy God and then reached out to take the hand of sinful humanity, He connected the two and said, "It is finished."

God wants to know you. That's why He revealed Himself on Sinai. He wants to have fellowship with you, but the only way you can know God is through Jesus Christ, the sinless sacrifice, who died for us on the cross. You can't move on to the other nine requirements of God until you settle this primary one.

CHAPTER TWO

Get Real!

"You shall not make for yourself an idol in the form of anything in heaven above, on the earth beneath, or in the waters below. You shall not bow down to them or worship them; for I, the Lord your God, am a jealous God, punishing the children for the sin of the fathers to the third and fourth generation of those who hate me, but showing love to a thousand generations of those who love me and keep my commandments."

Exodus 20:4-6

This is perhaps the most misunderstood of all the Ten Commandments. Some people have mistaken it to mean that artwork of any kind is a sin against God. Some have misunderstood this commandment to be speaking against the value of aesthetics in general. And yet, God later gave instructions to build the tabernacle fashioned with beautiful decorations (see Exodus 35:4ff). Actually, there were two beautiful statues of cherubim whose wings arched over the mercy seat covering the ark of the covenant. This prohibition is not against making a beautiful image; the prohibition is against bowing down and worshiping the work of our hands.

What Is Idolatry?

There are people today who think that because they do not make or worship statues or totem poles, they are not idolaters. However, any incorrect image of God can make us an idolater. In the New Testament, we learn that it is possible to become so greedy that the very act of "wanting more" can constitute idolatry. *"Put to death, therefore, whatever belongs to your earthly nature: sexual immorality, impurity, lust, evil desires, and greed, which is idolatry,"* (Colossians 3:5).

When we think of idolatry, we most often picture worshipers bowing down before some kind of man-made object. Indeed, this is a form of IDOL WORSHIP. We have a natural tendency to want to see or touch something so that we can know that it is real. That's why pagans built temples and statues. They crafted likenesses of their gods so they could carry this clear mental image of the appearance of their gods from place to place.

However, after thousands of years, we still prefer the same kind of "real" god as well. I heard about a little boy who got scared in the middle of the night. He ran into his parents' bedroom and yelled, "Daddy! Daddy! I'm scared! The boogie man is in my room!"

As most dads do, his dad said, "Son, there is no boogie man in here. Just go back to bed. Don't you know that God is in there with you?"

The little boy thought for a minute and said, "Yes, daddy, but I sure would rather have somebody with skin on."

Like that little boy, we *would* rather have a god that we could look at and hang onto. That's why it is so easy for us to prefer some IMAGE of God rather than the INVISIBLE God.

The Defects of Material Images

When we speak of a material image of God, we may conjure up the idea of a bronzed grinning Buddha, a wooden totem pole, a strange-shaped rock or perhaps even a golden crucifix. In the movie, *Cool Hand Luke*, Paul Newman is driving along in his 1956 Chevrolet, and on his dashboard, he had a plastic figure of Jesus. As he drove down the highway, he would sing, "I don't care if it rains or freezes as long as I've got my plastic Jesus." Obviously, that's a material image. It's not too uncommon in rural areas to pass cars that have a figure of Jesus or Mary on the dashboard. That image makes it easier for the driver to "picture" (imagine) what their God looks like.

The weakness of any material image is that it can never come close to capturing the greatness and majesty of the true and living God. Any attempt to represent God with an idol actually reduces God. Even the most beautiful idol or image just can't approach the character of our amazing God.

Here's a simple illustration. Have you ever seen a poster or a television program about Mount Rushmore in South Dakota? No television screen, poster or even wide screen movie can capture the majesty and beauty of that massive sculpture. The four faces of George Washington, Thomas Jefferson, Abraham Lincoln and Bill Clinton (just checking to see if you are paying attention)...and Theodore Roosevelt, have been chiseled from Mount Rushmore. Each face is almost 100 feet tall. Any image (or picture) of Mount Rushmore only reduces it. Seeing it in person is the ONLY way to experience its wonder and majesty.

What if I gave you a handful of clay and asked you to make a representation of Mount Rushmore? You might try, but you would not be able to come close to demonstrating the greatness of Mount Rushmore. Your little clay replica would actually be an insult to the real thing—no matter how many they sold in the souvenir shops.

That's exactly why God forbids worship of any "image." No material image can truly represent Him, and any attempt to do so actually insults His greatness. To put it simply, a material image is just a BAD PICTURE of God.

There once was a rather unattractive woman who was upset over the proofs that her photographer had provided of her photo shoot. She stomped into the shop, her proofs wadded up in her hand, and said to the photographer, "Mister, these pictures just don't do me *justice*."

The overworked photographer responded, "Lady, you don't need justice; you need *mercy*."

There is not a picture, image or statue on earth that could ever do God justice. He doesn't want us to be confused by looking at these poor pictures of Him.

You could probably do a better job describing Rushmore using only your words. Those listening to you could let their imagination envision it bigger than any picture you could show them. We often use the expression, "A picture is worth a thousand words." However, when it comes to the nature of God, He has chosen to use thousands of words (the Bible) rather than any one picture.

Representation or Reminder

The primary danger of using material images in worship is that these images may come to *represent* God instead of *reminding* us of God. The Bible does not forbid symbols, but it does forbid idols. What is the difference? A symbol reminds us of God, but an idol or an image may be used to represent God. When we cross over the line to something that represents God, instead of just reminding us of God, we've entered into the sin of idolatry.

Consider this example. Imagine a wife attending a party with her husband, making small talk in a corner, when a beautiful young woman walks by. The wife looks at her with a little twinge of envy and comments, "She is a beautiful girl." Ever thoughtful, the husband looks at the beautiful stranger and looks at wife and responds, "Yes, she is. And you know, dear, she reminds me of you." What a way to make his wife feel good about herself!

However, let's just imagine that 15 minutes later the wife walks down the hall and opens a closet door to get her coat, only to discover her husband with that beautiful young woman in his arms. He pulls away quickly, but it is obvious that he has been kissing her. Stuttering and stammering, he quickly explains, "I know this doesn't look good, but listen, dear, I wasn't doing anything wrong. I was just letting her represent you. Remember, I told you that she reminded me of you. When I was kissing her, it was if I was kissing you!"

Ladies, if you would believe that, I've got some oceanfront property in Abilene, Texas that I want to sell to you. Of course, you wouldn't accept his excuse. No self-respecting woman wants another girl to represent her to her man. She might say, "I don't mind somebody reminding you of me, but I won't tolerate your letting another woman represent me!" God is saying the same thing in this second commandment.

Can I Wear a Cross or Crucifix?

A cross or crucifix that you wear around your neck might be a harmless symbol, but if you ever begin to worship, kiss or assign some magical power to it, you've crossed over the line, and it is no longer a symbol; it is an idol. I think some people can break the second commandment with a crucifix. Why? A crucifix can't picture all the greatness of the Lord Jesus Christ. To some, it may be just a simple reminder of the death of Jesus—to others it may become an icon that they bow before or kiss.

Let me use a superfluous example of the subtle danger of a crucifix. Yes, Jesus died for us, but the truth of the glorious gospel is this: He didn't just die. He is alive again. Instead of wearing that crucifix, perhaps you should also wear a tiny replica of an empty tomb around your neck. But, wait a minute; He ascended into heaven so you ought to wear a necklace with a small tower on the Mount of Olives, the point from which He ascended. He is seated on the throne of heaven and He will return to earth some day. Why don't you also wear a throne around your neck? Why stop there? Jesus said, "I am the door." So let's put a small door on a chain around your neck. He also said, "I am the Bread of heaven," so... Well, maybe you have the picture now. Before long, you are going to be bending over and dragging the floor—you'll have so many symbols around your neck. As wonderful as the sacrifice of Jesus on the cross is, even a crucifix cannot capture the scope of the greatness of Jesus.

I hope you have the point—a material image can't capture God's character. There is a majesty and a mystery related to God that can't be reduced to some man-made figure or the greatest natural beauty on earth. God is bigger than any of our images.

A Faulty Mental Image of God Is Idolatry

In addition to material images, a poor mental image can cause us to violate this commandment. When you close your eyes and try to imagine God, what image do you project onto the screen of your consciousness? Be careful that you don't begin to worship that mental image alone. In fact, I challenge you to get rid of that picture because there is no one picture that will capture the greatness of

God. There is a mystery to the greatness of God. That's why the Bible says, *"Great is the mystery of godliness,"* 1 Timothy 3:16.

God says in Isaiah 55:9, *"As far as the heavens are above the earth, so high are my thoughts above your thoughts and my ways above your ways."* God is letting us know that it is impossible for our feeble minds to comprehend His mighty character.

Our finite minds quickly become overloaded when we try to conceive of the infinite, invisible God. We can't even grasp the breadth of eternity. Try imagining a line that represents eternity. How far is your time line? Double it. Triple it. Quadruple it. Multiply it by ten. Multiply it by a million to the millionth power... and you still haven't even made a scratch on the true line of infinity. Our brains can't contain eternity—much less an eternal God.

If you think you have an accurate idea of what God looks like and what God acts like, then you have actually put God into the tiny box of your own intelligence. You have just reduced the infinite God to the size of your human imagination—and that's a poor mental image of God. You need to knock the sides, bottom and top off your box and stop trying to stuff God into the confines of your imagination. To assume that you can have a correct mental image of God that captures the totality of his greatness is to elevate your minds to the level of God - and that is idolatry.

Our Minds Are Only One-Dimensional

Here's another fault of mental images of God. Our minds can only focus one on dimension of God's character at a time. Someone has said, "The human mind is an amazing organ. It starts working the moment you are born and doesn't stop until you stand up in front of a crowd to speak!" Indeed, the human brain is one of the most complex computers ever designed. Our memory capacity is amazing; it's just that most of what we know is hidden in the files of our subconsciousness. It only takes a picture, or the lyrics of an old song to surface some of this memory capacity. However, our minds have one limiting factor—we can't really focus on two or more images simultaneously. We are limited to one image at a time. Like the popular software program, we can have many "windows" open on our screen at one time, but we can only work on one screen at a time. We can switch back and forth quickly, but we can only look at them one at a time. This quirk of our minds ought to convince us that our mental images of God are inadequate because we can only consider one attribute of God at a time. And the great God cannot be confined to only one attribute.

You may have a mental image of God as some angry, overbearing, cosmic police officer who is just waiting to catch you doing something wrong so He can punish you. If that's your image of God, it is an incomplete and incorrect picture of God. Alternatively, you may picture God as some elderly, hard-of-hearing, senile grandfather type. You see Him wearing a long white robe with a flowing white beard. He is sitting on a heavenly rocking chair oblivious to our everyday life. Both of these pictures can mislead people because both are incorrect. Simply stated, you CANNOT create an accurate mental image of God. He's just too big for our little minds.

In Isaiah 40:25, God asks this question: *"'To whom will you compare me? Or who is my equal?' says the Holy One."* The correct answer is: **God, You are so great you can't be compared to anyone or anything that my mind can ever imagine.**

Beware the Dangers of Idle Worship
While we are discussing the sin of IDOL worship, we must also consider the sin of idle worship. That is, worship practiced by those who approach God with apathy or complacency. In order for worship to be acceptable to God, the OBJECT of our worship must be correct, but also the ATTITUDE of the worshiper must be right. When we direct our worship to the wrong object (anything or anyone other than God), that constitutes IDOL worship. However, it is possible to direct our worship to God, but fail to worship with the proper attitude—that's IDLE worship.

What does God say about idle worship? Idle worship arouses His jealousy. In Exodus 20:5, God says, *"I am the Lord your God. I am a jealous God."* You may stumble over that statement because you know that "God is love." And you also know that the Bible says, "Love is not jealous" (1 Corinthians 13:4). So how, then, can God be jealous? Doesn't that sound contradictory? Not at all. When the Bible says, "love is not jealous," it means that we are not to be jealous **of** someone that we love, but we should be jealous **for** those we love. That's how God can be a jealous God and still be a God of love.

Here's another way to understand this. My wife, Cindy, is a great communicator who addresses women's groups all over the country. When I am speaking somewhere, a woman will often come up to me afterwards and comment on my wife's speaking skills. If I was jealous of her, I might feel insecure and wonder if she thought my wife was a better speaker than I am (she is, by the way). Of course, I'm not jealous **of** her, so I am always happy to hear people compliment her. Nevertheless, because I love her, I am jealous **for** her. I don't want anyone else occupying the place in her heart that is reserved for me. If I find anyone trying to take my place, I will express a great deal of "righteous indignation" indeed!

God is not jealous of us; He is jealous for us. That means He won't tolerate any competition for our allegiance and devotion. If we sense that our spouse or significant other's love for us has become complacent, then we become jealous. When we are guilty of idle worship, God's jealousy is aroused as well.

The consequences of improper worship are severe. God makes a harsh promise in Exodus 20:5. He says, *"I am a jealous God, punishing the children for the sins of the fathers to the third and fourth generation of those who hate me."* Is this the warning of an angry God who holds a grudge for generations? It actually is an observation about the kind of worship heritage each generation leaves for the next generation. There are very serious consequences that naturally follow when we do not worship correctly. Not only does it affect us, it affects our children and subsequent generations.

What Are You Teaching Your Children about Worship?

The story of King Uzziah perfectly illustrates what God is saying here. Uzziah was a competent king. However, he possessed a serious character flaw: pride. He watched as the priests went into certain parts of the temple that were off-limits to others—even to the king. Dismayed that the KING could not go anywhere he pleased, one day he ventured into the restricted areas of the temple.

The priests warned him. Azariah the High Priest said, *"It is not right for you, Uzziah, to burn incense to the Lord. That is for the priests, the descendants of Aaron, who have been consecrated to burn incense. Leave the sanctuary, for you have been unfaithful; and you will not be honored by the Lord God"* (2 Chronicles 26:18).

Like Jim Carrey's character in The Mask, Uzziah said in essence, "Somebody stop me!" They didn't stop him—God did. *"While he was raging with the priest in their presence before the incense altar in the Lord's temple, leprosy broke out on his forehead"* (26:19). Uzziah turned and left the temple, and the Bible says that he never returned to the temple again. He never attended church again. In fact, he went to his palace and finally died of leprosy. Notice, that's Generation One.

Enter Generation Two.

Uzziah's son, Jotham, was a good king, but he never went to church and never went to the temple. His reason is a familiar one— the "church people" mistreated his daddy and made his daddy mad. I've met dozens of modern "Jothams" who avoid going to church for no other reason than their daddy never went. That's Generation Two.

Enter Generation Three, Jotham's son, Ahaz. He never went to the temple, and not only that, he shut it down. He took the objects of worship from the temple and used them in the worship of pagan fertility gods. He became a rank pagan. What is happening here? The first generation initiates idle worship; the second generation doesn't worship at all, and by the third generation, wickedness replaces worship.

It's sad to see what happened to happened in the fourth generation. Ahaz was so immersed in pagan worship that he sacrificed his own sons (see 2 Chronicles 28:3) Where did this tragedy start? It started with a man three generations earlier who did not worship God the correct way (idle worship). The way one generation worships will affect the next several generations (Exodus 20:5).

Parents and grandparents, your children will inherit a spiritual heritage of worship from you. If you don't worship correctly, sincerely, and faithfully, then it will affect your future generations. That's the danger of idle worship.

What Is Ideal Worship?

This commandment has a positive side—the delight of *ideal* worship. Ideal worship is correct in its DIRECTION (the object of our worship is God), and it is proper in its PRACTICE (the correct attitude). When you discover what IDEAL worship is, you will find that worship is a DELIGHT, not a duty. You will have such joy, rejoicing in the Lord.

Look at the last thing God says in this commandment in Exodus 20:6, "*. . .but showing love to thousands who love me.*" God desires our love and our worship. When He receives it, He responds by showing love to those who love Him. Don't you desire to be one of the thousands to whom God is constantly showing His love? Here's how you can be in that number.

The key to ideal worship is found in John 4:23. Jesus has entered into a discussion with a Samaritan woman who asks Him a question about proper worship. Jesus says to her, "*A time is coming and now has come when the true worshipers will worship the Father in spirit and in truth, for they are the kind of worshipers the Father seeks.*"

You can't see, touch or taste God—He is Spirit. You can't connect with God on the physical level. Only when your spirit connects with God's Spirit can true worship occur. To worship God in **Spirit** and in **truth** means that we worship Him in the right attitude (spirit) and in the right way (truth). God is actually looking around for people who will worship Him this way. The Bible says in 2 Chronicles 16:9, "*For the eyes of the Lord range throughout the earth to strengthen those whose hearts are fully committed to Him.*" God is searching for people who will worship Him properly. What does He do when He finds them? He shows His love to them. (Exodus 20:6)

Whenever we gather to worship, it is as if the Spirit of our Father is searching throughout the room, silently asking, "Are you really going to worship me? Are you going to love me?" What does He find when He looks at you?

Our Father Loves to Be Loved

I learned more in five minutes about the nature of God by being a father for five minutes than I learned in all my years in theological training. When I laid eyes on my daughters, I was overwhelmed with love for them. Even though they sometimes awoke me from sleep and demanded a lot of my time and attention—I still cherished them. And when they were old enough to reach their arms out to me and express their love to me—whew! I was humbled to begin to understand that God loves me the same way I love my daughters and much more! Knowing if He felt like I did when my children showed their love to me, I came to see that the best thing I could give God was my love and adoration.

Throughout the years, my daughters have returned my love. They have often asked me for things, and if I believed that those things would be good for them, I would try to honor their requests. However, there were times when they would just send me a note or card and tell me how much they loved me. They didn't want anything; they just wanted to say they loved me. Those are the times I was MOST blessed to be a father.

Transfer that idea to God the Father. Have you ever gone to worship and just told Him how much you love Him—without asking for anything? When was the last time you sat down and wrote a letter to the Lord (or prayed a prayer to Him) telling Him how awesome He is and how blessed you are to be part of His family? God responds positively in the same way any parent would.

But Doesn't God Love Everybody?

Exodus 20:6, says, *". . . but showing love to a thousand generations of those who love me and keep my commandments."* Doesn't God love everybody? Absolutely. Doesn't God love even those people who do not worship him correctly? Absolutely. However, please notice that there is a difference between God's loving someone and God's SHOWING LOVE to someone. That's the promise of Exodus 20:6; that He will SHOW love to those who worship Him correctly. Someone has said, "God has no favorites, but He has always had intimates." God desires our love, and He deserves our obedience. How do we SHOW our love to God? By just telling Him? There's a better way. In the last part of Exodus 20:6, He speaks of, *"...those who love me and keep my commandments."* In John 14:15, He says,

"If you love me you will obey what I command." You can't say you love God unless you are willing to obey Him ... in everything. Notice the order. He doesn't say, "Obey me and love me." He says, "Love me and obey me." **Worship** must come before **work**, but worship that doesn't lead to work is not real worship. Worship is empty unless we respond by obeying the Lord Jesus Christ.

One Thing Is Necessary

Remember the encounter that Jesus had with Mary and Martha (Luke 10:38-42)? Martha was in the kitchen, working for Jesus while Mary was sitting at the feet of Jesus just fellowshipping with Him as He talked to her. Martha thought the best way to show her love for Jesus was to work for Him in the kitchen. She was so convinced of this correct way to worship that she began to resent the idea that Mary was just sitting at Jesus' feet. I can imagine that after she dramatically banged a few pots and pans together to get attention, she stomped out of the kitchen wiping her hands on her ever-present hand towel to speak her mind. In this passage, she confronts Jesus and says, "Lord, tell Mary to come back here and help me."

Jesus didn't condescendingly say, "Mary, get out there and help her right now." No. We need to hear the reply of Jesus because He teaches us about the priority of worship over work. He looked at Martha and with a voice full of love, said, "Martha, Martha, you are worried and upset about many things, but only one thing is needed. Mary has chosen what is better, and it will not be taken away from her." (Luke 10:41-42) What is the "one thing" Jesus mentioned? It is spending time with God, developing personal intimacy with Him—*that* is worship.

Before the great violinist, Fritz Chrysler died in 1962, he learned of a rare Stradivarius violin that was in the possession of an English collector. With some outside financial backing, Chrysler offered the collector an astronomical price for the instrument.

However, the Englishman replied, "I'm sorry; it is not for sale at any price."

Fritz Chrysler, taken aback, countered by saying, "I am willing to give any price; just name the price. I have backers who are willing to pay."

Again, Chrysler gave the same reply. "The violin is part of a collection. It is not for sale at any price."

Finally, when Fritz Chrysler realized he wasn't going to change the man's mind, he made another request. "Well, would you at least allow me to play it once?"

After a moment of hesitation, the violin collector agreed. He took it from the case and handed it to Fritz Chrysler. The virtuoso performer lovingly brushed off the dust and tuned the strings. He gently placed the instrument under his chin, closed his eyes and began to play a selection of Brahms' compositions, not knowing that Brahms was the collector's favorite composer. He played for about 10 minutes, then said, "Thank you," and handed it back to the owner, whose face was wet with tears.

The Englishman took the violin and then gave it back to Chrysler. "It's yours." He said, "You are the master, and you alone deserve this instrument." He gave it without cost to the one who could play it so beautifully.

When I think of that story, I think of worship. Jesus Christ is the only One able to make anything beautiful out of our out-of-tune lives. Instead of stubbornly holding onto our own ideals and plans for our lives, we ought to say, "Lord, you are the Master. Here, I give you all that I have and all that I am." That's the kind of worship God deserves and desires.

CHAPTER 3

Watch Your Mouth

"You shall not misuse the name of the Lord your God for the Lord will not hold anyone guiltless who misuses his name." "Do not speak it in an empty sense or do not take it in vain." (Hebrew)

Exodus 20:7

S ome old laws are foolish and sound funny when you read them now. I've been told that these laws are actually on the books in some cities and states:

- In Pine Island, Minnesota, there is a law that says a man must remove his hat when he meets a cow.
- In Pocatello, Idaho, it is against the law to walk around looking "peeved and dejected." (I think that is a great law!)
- In Berea, Ohio, there is a law that states that every animal on the streets after dark must wear a tail light.
- A Michigan state law says that crocodiles may not be tied to fire hydrants.

- In Detroit, it is against the law to fall asleep in a bathtub.
- In Natchez, Mississippi, elephants are not permitted to drink beer.
- In Owensboro, Kentucky, if a woman wants to buy a hat, her husband must try it on first.
- In Kentucky a law says that a wife must have her husband's permission to move the furniture around the house.

Although these foolish and antiquated laws make us laugh, when God gave His ten moral requirements, it was no laughing matter. The first two laws are rather difficult for modern Americans to understand. Most of us feel confident we're not worshiping images or false gods, but when we talk about taking God's name in vain, it gets our attention. We have either done this, or we have heard it done more times than we care to admit. You may feel proud because you have never uttered an expletive that contains God or Jesus. However, like the other laws, you must dig below the surface to discover the full impact of this commandment. Many people have been guilty of violating the third commandment without even realizing it. Although profanity or cursing does violate this commandment, we can also violate it in other ways.

What's in a Name Anyway?

In the Bible, God's character links to His name. We have already discussed the mystery and power of the name YHWH. In our American culture, names don't really demonstrate character. We use names only to identify people. The Federal government knows us as a taxpayer ID number. The state knows us by our driver's license number. We might as well be a number because a number actually does a better job of identifying us sometimes. Others may share our name, but not our Social Security number. We just use names as convenient labels.

For several years, Gerber Baby Products surveyed the names of new babies. In the 1950s, the most popular names for baby girls were Mary, Elizabeth, Barbara, Dorothy and Helen. It's interesting to see how different generations prefer different names. In fact, Gerber Products tell us that the names that were popular in the 1950s are not used frequently today. The most common girl names in the 90s were Jennifer, Amanda, Ashley, Melissa, Nicole, Lauren and Megan.

In the 50s, the most popular names for boys were: John, William or Bill, Charles, James and George. In the 90s, the most popular names were Matthew, Jonathan, Bryan, Jason, Christopher, Andrew and Ryan. It really doesn't matter because when most parents name a child, they are just searching for a name that sounds good or is a family name.

In Bible times, every name carried a message. They were more than just numbers to distinguish and identify people; they said something about the person. Jacob and Esau were twin sons born to Isaac and Rebecca. Esau, the firstborn, was covered with red hair, so he was given a name that means "hairy." Jacob was born holding on to the heel of his older brother, so his parents gave him the name Yacob, which means "grabber." That name came to describe the personality of Jacob because for much of his life, he was a grabber. He grabbed for things that were not rightfully his. He grabbed for Esau's birthright. Later, when he had a wrestling encounter with an angel, he grabbed onto the angel and wouldn't let him go. God said, "No longer is your name Grabber. Because your character will change, your name must change." God gave Jacob a new name— Israel, which means "Prince of God."

When the Jewish scribes were copying the Old Testament scriptures, it was a meticulous process. When they came to the four-consonant name for God, YHWH, they would pause in their copying. They would leave the manuscript and fast and pray for at least 24 hours. Then they would go through a ritual cleansing in a mikvah, which was like a ceremonial bath. Then they would put on brand new garments. Only after all of this would they then sit down and take a new quill, never used before, and write those four Hebrew consonants. After writing those four consonants, they would take that quill and destroy it, so it would never write another word. They would get up, put the old clothes on again, pick up the original quill and continue copying. Six thousand times in copying the Old Testament, they had to stop and go through that ritual. They did that because the name of God was such a special, holy name. That's why God has warned us about misusing His name. When you speak the name of God, you bring His character into focus. If you do not afford His name the honor that His character demands, you are taking His name in vain.

Profanity Is Prohibited

One of the most commons ways that God's name and character are insulted is by vulgar speech, or profanity. The word "profanity" comes from two Latin words, *Pro Fanitas* which means "out of the temple" or "outside from that which is decent or good." When you utter profanity, you take something holy, special and different and make it common and unclean. Millions of people are guilty on a daily basis of impugning God's holy character by profaning His name. They are actually praying an unholy prayer when they speak for God to "damn" someone or something. They are praying an unholy prayer when they ask someone to "go to hell" or are taking some common, dirty, filthy, profane word and applying it to someone. They are taking those matters that ought to be only holy or spiritual and are making them angry, unkind and hateful. That is profanity.

Some people wonder if they can use another curse word, as long as they don't use the name of God or Jesus. A person who loves God does not use profanity—period. As parents, we find it difficult to shield our children from that sort of vile language. As the father of two precious daughters, I found that it was impossible to shield them totally from being exposed to profanity. I can remember telling my girls when we would hear a profanity uttered on television or in a movie, "Girls, Christians don't use that kind of language." Later, both girls came to me saying, "Wait a minute. I know some Christians who talk like that." I had to change what I was teaching my daughters. I now say, "Committed Christians do not use that kind of language. Spirit-filled Christians do not use that kind of language. Fully devoted followers of Jesus Christ don't talk that way."

God Hates Vulgar Speech

People who use profanity usually fall under two categories. First, there are those who don't realize that profanity is an affront to God, and they curse out of ignorance. God doesn't want us to speak that way—but they just don't know it yet. Yet there are others who claim to be a Christian, and they know that God is not pleased with their vocabulary, but it seems that they cannot control it. The truth is that they **can** control it if they **choose** to. Many "Christians" who use profanity six days a week, will never curse when they are in church. Think about it. There's nothing holy about a church building. If they can refrain from profanity for one or two hours on Sunday morning, they can refrain from it the rest of the days during the week. They can stop it if they desire to stop it.

I have a vivid memory of the danger of profanity. When I was a young boy, I idolized my dad. My father was a rough, tough, good ol' guy. He was a Christian, but his vocabulary wasn't clean all the time. He was a forester and worked with outdoorsmen, and I heard a lot of language that I didn't understand. I'll never forget that time when I was only five years old and only as tall as the top drawer of my chest of drawers. I was fighting with this drawer one morning, trying to get it open. I had heard my dad talk, so right there in the presence of my mom, I uttered the "d" word. I said, "I just can't get this (blank) drawer open."

After her initial shock, my mother was outraged. She jerked me up, dragged me to my dad and asked, "Do you know what your son just said?"

My dad was ready to administer a little punishment to me and demanded, "Son, where did you hear that kind of language?"

Softly, I replied, "From you, Daddy." I think I remember that experience because it was the first time I remember escaping punishment. I never heard my dad utter any kind of word like that again. He consciously tried to control his language around his children.

A Feeble Mind Needs Profanity
A wise person once said, "Profanity is the attempt of a feeble mind to express itself forcefully." When I was a teenager, I was a hypocrite about profanity, because there was a certain setting and a certain group of friends with whom I would curse. When I showed up for my Sunday school class or worship service, I never used that

kind of language. I never spoke like that around my parents. I soon saw, however, that I had to have some consistency in my life and in my vocabulary.

The Bible says in James 3:10 says, *"Out of the same mouth comes cursing and praise to God. This should not be."* I'm praying that if you have a problem with occasional profanity, that God will bring you under conviction even as you are reading this sentence. You must decide whether you are going to use your mouth to praise God or to curse—to do both makes you inconsistent. When you ask God to damn someone or something, that's breaking the third commandment. At this point you may be thinking, "I may do that sometimes, but I'm not serious when I say that." However, that's precisely the violation of this commandment; you **say** it, but you don't **mean** it. This is what it means to misuse the name of the Lord, to take his name in vain.

Empty Speech Violates God's Law

You may still be thinking that you are doing pretty well in this area because, for you, profanity is not a problem. You must realize that there is another way to violate this commandment. Not only does vulgar speech violate this law, but vain (empty or meaningless) speech breaks it as well. In fact, this practice probably violates the third commandment more often than simple cursing or profanity.

Did you know that when you utter a prayer and you are not sincere in your prayer, you are misusing the name of God? It can be as simple as praying "God is great; God is good. Let us thank Him for our food." If you are not really, sincerely thanking God, you are misusing His name because you don't mean what you are saying about God.

Before our high school football team took the field, the team would huddle up with our heads together and say the Lord's Prayer. Isn't it funny that when football players put on pads and helmets, they get tough and talk differently? We wouldn't pray the prayer as we usually do, in a normal voice. We would use a deep, husky voice and chant the phrases in a crescendo of intensity, until we got to the last part, "For thine is the kingdom and the power and the glory forever, Amen!" It was as if we were saying, "Now let's go kill those guys."

I have already confessed to the Lord that every time I prayed that prayer in high school, I was violating the third commandment because I didn't mean a word of that prayer. I was just saying it by rote. It was simply a pre-game ritual, not a sincere prayer.

You don't have to be on a football team to make the same mistake. You can stand in church and recite a prayer like that, and if you are not sincere, you take God's name in vain. You must constantly examine yourself when you are praying a familiar prayer to make sure you are really talking to God, not just reciting familiar words.

Are You Sinning As You Are Singing?

Another way this law is broken is by empty praise. Many people come to church, open a hymn book and start mouthing the words to a song they have sung dozens of times. It's possible to be sinning even as you are singing if you are not concentrating on being sincere in your praise. There are so many wonderful hymns of faith that I love to sing. One of my favorites says, "Take my life and let it be, consecrated Lord for thee." If you have ever stood up and mouthed those words, but not sincerely offered yourself to the Lord, you are speaking in vain. The third verse of that beautiful hymn says, "Take my silver and my gold, not a mite would I withhold." If you've ever sung that out loud only to hang on to your money, silver and gold with all your might instead of saying, "Lord, it's all yours"—you have just violated the third commandment. You are taking His name in vain, because you are saying and singing something that you don't mean.

Do You Mean What You Say about Jesus?

Another way to sin is by making an empty (vain) profession. Jesus said, *"Why do you call me Lord, Lord and you don't do the things I say?"* (Luke 6:46). You can utter the words "Jesus is my Lord," but if your lifestyle says otherwise, you are taking His name in vain.

Have you noticed that many people are wearing crosses, and these emblems have no relation to a personal faith in Jesus. You see rock stars with crosses around their necks, in their earlobes, noses and everywhere they can put them, but this jewelry has absolutely nothing to do with their belief in Jesus Christ. Anytime we do something like that, it is an empty profession of our faith, and it is violating the third commandment. Anytime we claim to be Christians, but our lives do not live up to what we are saying, our lives become a violation of this commandment. These insincere, hollow displays are ways we can break this commandment.

C.S. Lewis once said, "The greatest cause of atheism in the world today is Christians who profess Jesus with their lips but deny Him with their lifestyles." These hypocritical actions are what an unbelieving world finds simply incredible. Christians who sing, "Oh, how I love Jesus" on Sunday, but crucify Christ in their business on Monday have driven people away from God. Even an unbelieving world can spot a hypocrite. They are saying to us, "You are a fake. You are misusing the name of the Lord."

Always Look for the Positive
Some people stumble over all the "thou shalt nots" in the Bible. They think that the Bible is such a negative document. However, anytime God says not to do something, you should quickly look for the good, positive actions you can take. For instance, in the Garden of Eden, when God said, "Don't eat from this one tree," He was saying, "Eat of all the other trees, but don't eat this one tree." That's a positive approach.

The positive side of this command is that we should always speak the name of God in the correct way. In Exodus 20:7, He is saying, "Use my name, honor my name, respect my name, exalt my name." There is a positive side to it, so don't look at the Ten Commandments as God's slapping your wrist saying, "Don't you do that." He is saying, "Help yourself to happiness by using my name reverently, correctly, and with respect." Anytime you use God's name, you call His character into focus. When you don't acknowledge His character or you impugn His character, you violate this commandment.

Several years ago, I was preaching at the great Olive Baptist Church in Pensacola, Florida. A man came up to me after about the third night of the revival and said, "Dykes, huh? I used to know a guy by the name of Dykes from Panama City. We grew up together, but I lost track of him because when he was 13, his dad died, and he quit school so he could work in the sawmill to help support his mother and sisters. Later, he joined the Navy, and I haven't heard from him since. Maybe he's related to you. His name was Orlo Dykes."

Long before he said the name, I could tell from that description that he was talking about my dad. I said, "Yes. That was my dad."

He said, "Really? It's a small world, isn't it? You know, your dad was a great guy."

I really appreciated that. This man, who was a total stranger to me, brought my father's name into focus. Then, because he knew some good things about him, he exalted his character by saying nice things. What if this same guy had said, "Did you ever know a guy named Orlo Dykes? He was sure a sorry scoundrel"? His estimation of my father's character would have insulted me!

In the same way, we ought to bring God's name into focus on a regular basis by saying something positive and complimentary about His character. Jesus best reveals God's name and His character. Philippians 2:9 says, *"Therefore God exalted him (Jesus) to the highest place and gave him the name that is above every name..."*

What can we find that is positive in the name of Jesus? For example, He is our source of strength. Proverbs 18:10 says, *"The name of the Lord is a strong tower; the righteous run to it and are safe."* Whenever you face trouble in life - whether it is the death of a loved one; or a sudden accident; or a long, lingering illness, the **only** name that can give you strength to cope is the name of Jesus. If you are going through a family crisis - perhaps your mate has left you, or your kids are rebelling, or someone has broken your heart - only the name of Jesus can give you strength to cope. During your greatest times of need, it's not the name of the President, the Pope or the preacher who will deliver you - it's only the name of Jesus. Don't take this precious name in vain.

What Is the Lord's Name?

In the Old Testament, God revealed His name as YHWH. However, we can know Him by a new name. Romans 10:13 says, "For whoever calls upon the name of the Lord will be saved." Notice it DOESN'T say, "For everyone who calls on the Lord will be saved." That's what most people think - just call on the Lord. But it clearly says you must call on the **name** of the Lord to be saved.

You'll hear many people talk about "the Good Lord." They say, "Oh yeah, I know the Good Lord. Me and the Good Lord, we're tight." Or they talk about "the Man Upstairs." You'd better be careful, because it's not "the Good Lord" who will save you; nor is it "the Man Upstairs." The *Lord* has a name and His name is Jesus. That's the only name you can call upon to be saved. In Acts 4:12, we read, *"Salvation is found in no one else, for there is no other name under heaven given to men by which we must be saved."* Jesus Christ was born of a virgin, lived a sinless life, died a substitutionary death for you, was buried, resurrected, ascended into heaven and is coming again—that's the only name that will get you into heaven. Don't take that name lightly.

Suppose there comes a time when you stand before heaven's gate, and God asks, "Why should I let you into heaven?" Please don't say, "I was a member of New Life Church. Or don't say, "I was baptized." Don't say, "I gave money to the church." Say, "Because Jesus is my Lord." That's the *only name* that will gain you eternal access to heaven.

In the End, It's the Only Name That Matters

William Booth was the founder of the Salvation Army and a totally committed Christian. His wife, Catherine, was a tremendous believer, as well. In 1912, as William Booth lay on his deathbed, in the last hours of his physical life, some solicitors came to Catherine Booth and said, "Mrs. Booth, we are faced with a massive problem. The assets of the Salvation Army will be in question unless General Booth signs some legal papers about what will happen to the assets of the Salvation Army. Will you take these papers to General Booth and ask him to sign them?"

As William Booth breathed the last breaths of his life, Catherine came into his room and said, "Darling, you must sign these legal papers so that our property will be cared for in the right way." She put those papers before him and pointed to the places for him to sign. He signed six or seven times as she flipped the pages. Within a few hours, he was absent from the body, present with the Lord.

After the funeral, the solicitors began to look at those legal papers. On every line, William Booth had written "Jesus" instead of his own name. Why did he do that? I think it's because when we come to the end of our life, the only name that will mean anything to us is the name of Jesus. That's why God says that we should never misuse His name.

CHAPTER 4

R.I.P. without a Tombstone

"Remember the Sabbath day by keeping it holy. Six days you shall labor and do all your work, but the seventh day is a Sabbath to the Lord your God. On it you shall not do any work, neither you, nor your son or daughter, nor your manservant or maidservant, nor your animals, nor the alien within your gates. For in six days the Lord made the heavens and the earth, the sea, and all that is in them, but he rested on the seventh day. Therefore the Lord blessed the Sabbath day and made it holy."

Exodus 20:8-11

Would you like to "Rest In Peace" *before* you go to the cemetery? The title of this chapter reminds me of the story about a man who died and was buried. His wife assumed that they had plenty of money, so before the estate was settled, she spent a lot of her own money to purchase a nice tombstone that read: REST IN PEACE. After the attorney probated the will, she discovered that her husband had wasted all his money on gambling and bad investments. Instead of receiving money, the wife found that she actually owed a great deal of money to her late husband's creditors. This made her so angry that she took some of the money she had left and added three more words to the tombstone. Now it said: REST IN PEACE ....UNTIL I COME!

You really can Rest In Peace without a tombstone. This fourth requirement for America's survival is about how to rest. The word "Sabbath" means rest. God instituted the principle of the Sabbath because He knew that we would all need to set aside a day for rest and worship.

I have had the joy of being in Jerusalem numerous times on Friday afternoon. For the Jews, their Sabbath begins at sundown on Friday and lasts until sunset on Saturday. It is both amazing and refreshing to see the transformation that occurs in Jerusalem when the Sabbath begins. A curtain of serenity, tranquility and quietness falls over the Jewish part of this holy city. The hectic noise of busses, trucks and cars is replaced by silence on most of the streets. An eerie stillness replaces the constant drone of construction. And all of this happens in the more secular sections of Jerusalem.

In some sections of the city, where the very strict orthodox Jewish people live, a person may actually be arrested and punished if he or she walked into that section on the Sabbath. Cars that may mistakenly venture into the Orthodox neighborhoods are met with barricades and often become the target of rotten fruit thrown by the Jews who resent anyone who desecrates the Sabbath.

Even the modern hotels in Jerusalem have been built in accordance with the strict Sabbath laws. Since it is considered "work" to push an elevator button, each hotel has a "Sabbath elevator." For the 24 hours of the Sabbath, this elevator automatically stops on every floor - the door slowly opens and after a few moments, closes. If you are in a hurry, DON'T make the mistake of getting on the Sabbath elevator. Since activating an electric sensor is considered lighting a fire (forbidden on the Sabbath), the electric doors in these hotels are disarmed on the Sabbath. Having been in Jerusalem on the Sabbath, I understand how seriously the Jews regard this command. I have gained a deeper understanding of the value of the Sabbath to the Jewish people.

Should We Strictly Observe the Sabbath?
Christians are confused about exactly HOW the Sabbath law should

be observed today. Does this commandment forbid the opening of retail stores on Sunday? Should we go to football games, play golf or go fishing on Sunday? I hope you will follow along carefully as I hope to share some insight about how we should obey the fourth commandment.

It's easy to notice that of the Ten Commandments, God gives more information about the fourth commandment than to any of the others. The Hebrew word, *shabbat*, doesn't mean "seven" as some think. It is a word that literally means, "To cease, desist or stop." In our modern vernacular, it could mean, "to knock it off, chill out." It just means to **stop and be still**.

Which Day Is the Sabbath?

Are you breaking the fourth commandment? You can't know the answer to that question until you know which day is the Sabbath and what God requires of you concerning that day. There are basically **two incorrect interpretations** about the Sabbath that have caused generations of Christians to be confused and to feel unnecessary guilt:

(1) Christians must observe the Jewish Sabbath (Saturday).

Or

(2) Sunday has become the "Christian Sabbath."

Notice, I stated that BOTH of these interpretations are incorrect. If the first interpretation is true, then millions of Christians who worship on Sunday are terribly guilty and should be under the wrathful judgment of God.

You may be familiar with groups of Christians who worship on the Jewish Sabbath. The most familiar of all of these groups is the Seventh Day Adventist Church. They sincerely believe that Christians are still bound by the Sabbath commandment—and that means worship on Saturday.

Part of my spiritual heritage is in the Adventist church. My grandmother was married to a preacher in the Adventist church (they later formed the Christian Advent church which was a branch off the Seventh Day Advent church). There are also groups who call themselves Seventh Day Baptists. Other Christians call themselves Sabbatarians—Christians who observe worship on Saturday, because it is the seventh day, the Jewish Sabbath.

These groups generally say to the rest of us, "You folks are worshiping on the wrong day." Some of these sects are deep into biblical prophecy (David Koresh and the Branch Davidians were a splinter group of the Seventh Day Adventist Church). Some even go so far as to say that people who worship on Sunday are carrying the mark of the beast as found in the book of Revelation.

What about the Jewish Dietary Laws?
Many of these groups that insist that Saturday is the Sabbath also observe the dietary regulations of the Old Testament as well (see Leviticus 11). For this reason, they won't eat pork, shrimp or catfish because these foods are forbidden in the Levitical law. At least they are trying to be consistent in their understanding of the Old Testament law.

Are you sinning when you eat bacon or ham? Are you violating God's law if you don't worship on Saturday? Are you breaking this commandment if you push an elevator button on Saturday? Many folks have been made to feel guilty because they weren't obeying all these regulations of the Jewish Law. The answer for these questions is found in the New Testament.

Jesus Nailed Those Regulations to His Cross!
Relax, fellow believer, the New Testament states very clearly says that Christians are NOT bound by the Jewish Sabbath law. Read it for yourself: In Colossians 2:14-17, the apostle Paul is writing about the impact of the sacrificial death of Jesus and he says,

"Having canceled the written code (that means all of these laws that were added to the Torah) *with its regulations, that was against us that stood opposed to us; he* (Jesus) *took it away, nailing it to the cross."* Then verse 15 talks about *"having spoiled principalities and powers, he made a show of them openly."* Then it says, **"Therefore, do not let anyone judge you by what you eat or drink,**

or with regard to a religious festival, a New Moon celebration or a Sabbath day. These (meaning all these ceremonial ordinances) *are a shadow of the things that were to come; the reality, however, is found in Christ."*

Read it again. There was a large body of "regulations" or "ordinances" in the Old Testament. These regulations "stood against us." This means it was IMPOSSIBLE to keep every single law for every single day of a person's life. When Jesus died, He nailed those ordinances to His cross (along with our sin) and He "took them away." Included with this group of dietary regulations is the observance of a "Sabbath day."

Civil, Ceremonial or Moral Law?

To understand this point, you must consider that there are at least three kinds of law contained in the Old Testament. (1) **Civil Law** dealt with the government, calendar, and organization of the Jewish nation. (2) **Ceremonial Law** dealt with the temple sacrificial system and the Levitical requirements. (3) **Moral Law** addressed major issues of right and wrong for every person on earth - not just the Jews. The crucial point I want you to consider is: **We are no longer bound by the civil or ceremonial laws of the Old Testament - but we will always be required to obey God's moral law.**

Colossians 2:16 includes the Sabbath observance in the same category as the dietary regulations - a ceremonial law. This is a significant distinction about the fourth commandment, and if you don't recognize it, you will be confused for much of your life. The fourth commandment is the **only** one of the ten that is part of God's ceremonial law, not God's moral law.

What Is a Moral Law?

What, then, makes the other nine commandments part of God's moral law? Consider the commandment that prohibits murder. Before God gave the Ten Commandments, it was wrong for someone to murder someone else. It had **always** been wrong, and always **is** wrong. Although God had yet to give the Ten Commandments, Cain's murder of Abel was a sin against God - it violated His moral law. Consider the others - it was wrong to steal, even before God gave the Ten Commandments. He just confirmed it by stressing it again. Adultery, lying, stealing, idolatry and profanity - these were all considered sin - even before God gave the Ten Commandments on Sinai.

Now consider the Sabbath law. This requirement about the Sabbath never came into existence **until** God gave it to the nation of Israel at Sinai. Although God rested after six days of creation, He never commanded anyone else to do that until Sinai. We never read that Abraham, Isaac or Jacob ever observed the Sabbath. Of all the Ten Commandments, it is the only commandment that is mentioned as a sign of the Mosaic Covenant. Several scriptures make it clear that the Sabbath was a law God gave to the Israelites only, as a sign between God and the Israelites. It was **never** a general command to everyone else in the world. Consider Exodus 31:16-17 where God says: *"The Israelites are to observe the Sabbath, celebrating it for generations to come as a lasting covenant. It will be a sign between me and the Israelites forever."*

No Sabbath Command in the New Testament

You can find the other nine commandments repeated somewhere in the New Testament - but not the Sabbath Commandment. The fourth commandment is the only one of the ten that is not repeated as a law in the New Testament. Likewise, in the New Testament, there are only nine references to the word *shabbat*. Seven of the times, the scripture simply refers to the Jewish people who went to the synagogue on the Sabbath. The eighth reference is the one we have already examined in Colossians. The only other reference is in Hebrews 4, which will be examined later in this chapter.

At this point, you may be a little confused, so let's review. The New Testament makes it clear that Christians are not required to obey the ceremonial law of the Old Testament. The Sabbath Commandment is part of God's ceremonial law, given as a sign to the Nation of Israel. While this may be "new information" to you, I encourage you to search the Bible yourself. Get a good Bible dictionary and Concordance and read every line of Scripture that mentions the Sabbath. Remember, I've been addressing the first misunderstanding - that some say that Christians must worship on

Saturday, the Jewish Sabbath. But there's another misconception that is more widely held than the first.

Did Sunday Become the Christian Sabbath?

In 1979, I was serving as pastor of a small church in Central Alabama. It was a typical little town in the Bible belt, and all the stores were closed on Sunday. However, a large discount store moved into town, and we learned that it was going to be open on Sunday. Many Christians agree that we are not bound by the Old Testament regulations, and that we don't have to worship on Saturday. When asked the reason for this, they may say, "Oh, Sunday has become the Christian Sabbath." That's what I was taught for most of my life, and I just believed it without verifying it in Scripture. However, something happened that drove me to the Bible to see if this position is correct. In light of this new discount store's plans to be open on Sundays, I joined a group of concerned pastors who said, "We will not stand for it. This is wrong." We banded together to see what we could do about it.

Because I have always tried to follow the Bible, I began to search the scriptures to get ammunition to use against this "Sabbath-breaker" who planned to be open on the Christian Sabbath. I was in for a shock. I couldn't find a single scripture that referred to Sunday as the Christian Sabbath. I learned that early Christians worshiped on the "first day of the week," but they never called it the Sabbath. They even called Sunday "the Lord's day" perhaps because it was the day Jesus' resurrection was discovered - but no Sabbath regulations were attached to this day. And I couldn't find even a single scripture that addressed the issue of stores being open on Sunday. Boy, was I surprised! By the way, I invite you to perform the same scripture study. If you can find just one reference to Sunday as the Sabbath, then let me know!

Many of us grew up hearing that Sunday is the Christian Sabbath, and we are to observe Sunday the way the Jews observe their Sabbath. All my life, I've been hearing wonderful old saints of God pray on Sunday, "God, we thank you for this wonderful Sabbath day." At this point, you need to decide whether you are going to believe the Word of God or continue to embrace human traditions. To release some traditions is often painful, but Jesus said that sometimes our traditions make the Word of God of no effect.

The earliest Christians worshiped on the Jewish Sabbath because they were Jews. They went to the synagogue and temple and worshiped on the Sabbath day, but in Acts 2, we find that they actually worshiped every day. Later, it is obvious from several passages in the New Testament that Christians began to meet for a distinctively Christian service on the first day of the week. Perhaps it was because that was the day of the resurrection of Jesus. Most of the resurrection appearances of Jesus were on the first day of the week. In Revelation chapter 1, there is one reference to John the Apostle being "in the Spirit" on the Lord's Day. We don't know what day it was, but we've always assumed it was Sunday. Throughout the years, Christians have said, "Our distinctive day of worship, when we gather together as a community, is the first day of the week, the Lord's day.

However, how did that day ever become a Christian Sabbath? None of the early church fathers called it a Christian Sabbath. We hear about that for the first time in 313 A.D. when the Roman Emperor, Constantine, issued an edict that said the Roman Empire was going to be Christian. Instead of Christianizing paganism, he paganized Christianity!

Constantine issued another edict in 321 A.D. requiring the Roman empire to shut down on Sundays. Was it for a Christian reason? Listen to his words: "All judges, city people and craftsman shall rest on the venerable day of the Sun." Sun-day was the time that some of the pagan, mystery religions practiced their worship. Constantine was a political genius who "married" many pagan practices with the newfound Christian religion (look up "Christmas" in your encyclopedia to see why we celebrate it on December 25). Before long, it became a dogma of the Roman Catholic church that Sunday became the Christian Sabbath.

It's not in the Bible, but Catholic scholars admit freely that they changed Sunday into the Christian Sabbath.[ii] It wasn't something Jesus taught; it wasn't something the New Testament taught; it is something the Catholic church started doing.

During the 16th century, the Protestant Reformation "corrected" many of the unbiblical customs or rituals of the Roman Catholic Church. However, one of the doctrines they did not change was the Christian Sabbath. Many Protestants in America still base their Sunday beliefs on the teachings of the reformers. In 1643, the Westminister Confession, the confession of the Presbyterian Church, stated:

> *"God hath particularly appointed one day in seven for a Sabbath, to be kept holy unto Him, which from the beginning of the world, to the resurrection of Christ was the last day of the week, and from the resurrection of Christ was changed into the first day of the week, which in scripture is called the Lord's day, and Sunday is to be continued to the end of the world as the Christian Sabbath."*

Of course, not all traditions are bad, but if a tradition teaches something not verified in scripture, we need to consider it critically. When the Puritans came to America, they set up very strict regulations about Sunday being the Sabbath. That's where we get the term "blue laws." We often think of "blue laws" applying only to Sunday activities, but the Puritans wrote laws banning dancing, games and recreation as well. All of these strict regulations were called "blue laws." In the 60s, a number of states began to repeal the blue laws. The only "blue law" to survive for more than 300 years has been the law about Sunday closings. Many municipalities have long ignored the blue laws remaining on their books and choose not to enforce them.

Considering Sunday the Christian Sabbath is official dogma for the Catholic church, and it's right there in the Westminster Confession, but it's not in the Bible. With deep respect for the traditions of our Puritan ancestors, I must reject this teaching because it is foreign to Scripture. In light of all this, it's still possible for us to honor the spirit of the fourth commandment.

So, How Can I Keep the Fourth Commandment?
Much of what we've been taught about the Sabbath is based upon

man's tradition rather than the Word of God. This tradition has obscured a beautiful truth that we can discover about the Sabbath. Whereas the fourth commandment is not an immutable moral law of God like the other nine, it is a wonderful principle that New Testament Christians should observe. What is the difference? The Old Testament is a book of law; the New Testament is a book of love. The Old Testament is a book of commandments; the New Testament is a book of principles that enable us to experience abundant life. Although we are no longer living under the ceremonial or civil laws of Israel (thank God!), we still may obey the spirit of this fourth commandment that allows us to "rest' in peace.

A Rhythm of Work, Rest and Worship

Each of the Ten Commandments contains a positive aspect. When God says, *"Six days you shall work,"* He is speaking of the dignity and value of good hard work. The New Testament says in 2 Thessalonians 3:10, *"If a man will not work, he will not eat."* The New Testament teaches that it is good to work, but the spirit of the fourth commandment teaches that if all you ever do is work, you will be missing God's best for your life. Everyone needs to work, but everyone also needs to rest (Sabbath) or soon be overcome with weariness. Taking one day in seven to rest serves the purpose of renewing your strength.

We also need a weekly Sabbath to redirect our spirit. The example that God gives here in the fourth commandment is that on the seventh day, God rested. He created the Universe in six days. Some people say, "Do you really believe that God created the whole universe in six 24-hour periods?" I don't have any trouble believing that. I believe God could have created it in six 24-second periods. I believe God could have created the universe in six nano seconds. The point is not **how long** it took God to do it; the point is **how** He did it. He did it in six days because He was trying to teach us something very important. He was demonstrating to us the importance of after working six days, we need to take a day to rest and worship.

After six days of creation, do you think God said, "Whew! I'm tired! I've got to rest?" Of course not! God doesn't get tired. He doesn't lose His energy. The reason He "rested" was to teach us by example that we all must set aside time for rest and for worship, to redirect our spirit. That's the positive result of setting aside a day to worship and relax.

A Sabbath Will Recalibrate Your Spiritual Compass

I've been a private pilot for over thirty years. If you've ever been in the cockpit of a general aviation aircraft, you may notice that there are two compasses. A floating magnetic compass, usually mounted on the windshield, points to magnetic north. Pilots can't use that compass when they are climbing, turning, accelerating or decelerating because these forces affect it. The magnetic compass is reliable only when the aircraft is flying straight and level. Airplanes also have a Directional Gyro compass (DG). This compass on the instrument panel is run by a gyroscope, which means it isn't affected by the motion of the aircraft. This is the main compass that pilots use to fly a certain direction. However, this compass doesn't tune into magnetic north; it must be set by the magnetic compass. Throughout a flight, the pilot must recalibrate the DG to the magnetic compass, because the DG has a tendency to "recess" and it can become misleading. Any pilot who doesn't recalibrate the DG to the magnetic compass can miss his destination by miles!

The lesson I have learned from that is this: As I go through life, it is easy for my spirit to get out of line with God's desire for my life. If I don't constantly communicate with Him, I have a tendency to "drift" off course. Therefore, I must constantly be coming back and looking at God, focusing in on Him, concentrating on Him and His Word and then changing my life to fit His plan for me. That's the reason we all need a Shabbat. It's critically important that we gather with other people to worship God so that our spirits can be refreshed. We must set aside time to worship, or our lives will get out of control and out of direction.

I've heard people say, "I don't need to go to church. I don't need to read the Bible. I can just worship God out on the lake or in the deer stand. I can worship God on the golf course." Yet when we do not meet with the body of Christ to study God's Word, our lives and our spirits can recess, and before long, we think we are going in one direction when God wants another direction for us. We must constantly recalibrate our spirits to God's standard.

Another reason you need a Sabbath is to refresh your soul. In this rat race we call business, people often work 60-70 hours a week. Even when you put in those long hours, you still know that there is somebody out there who is working longer and harder than you are. You might expect that our technological advances have given us more leisure time, but exactly the opposite is true. Technology just allows us to do more, so people are working longer and harder to do more. People are more stressed out than ever before. I can recall a time when experts were saying we were heading toward a four-day workweek or a 30-hour workweek. Absolutely not! We are going in the other direction. The University of Chicago Business School surveyed a group of MBA's, and their average weekly hourly output for their job was 62 hours. Work! Work! Work! Stress! Stress! Stress! That's exactly why God knew that you would need a Sabbath.

Let Your Soul Catch up with Your Body
Once there was an African safari where some Americans were forging ahead into the jungle, using the natives to carry their burdens. They pressed on for ten straight days, never stopping to rest. After this hectic pace, they awoke one morning to find that the natives refused to carry their loads. The natives said, "We rest today. We must allow our souls to catch up with our bodies." That's the value of a day of rest, to let our souls catch up with our bodies.

In our modern society, our day of worship may not be the same as our day of rest. It certainly isn't for me. I pastor a growing congregation and I preach two times every Sunday morning and often again on Sunday night. Sunday is not a day of rest for me! It's one of the most tiring days of the week. For this reason, I try to consider Saturday as a day that I back off from a lot of work and try to relax my body, refresh my spirit and renew my soul.

How can you renew your spirit and truly experience a Sabbath? It's so easy to become weary and depleted. Isaiah 40 says, *"But they that wait upon the Lord shall renew their strength."* That doesn't mean that you sit around passively waiting for something to happen. To "wait upon" the Lord, means to be ready and willing to serve Him. Only when you do that can you experience the benefits of a Sabbath. According to this promise of God you will be so renewed that you will, *"soar on wings like eagles; run and not grow weary; walk and not faint."* Taking time to worship and rest must be among your top priorities each week.

A management consultant, teaching a course on time management, held a glass jar full of large rocks in front of the class. He asked, "Is the jar full?" Most of the class replied, "Yes." Then the consultant pulled out a bag of pebbles and poured them into the jar. As the pebbles settled in around the rocks, again he asked, "Is the jar full now?" This time, fewer agreed. Then he proceeded to take sand and pour it into the jar, sealing the crevices between the rocks and pebbles. "Is the jar full now?" By now, the class knew better than to say, "Yes." Finally, the consultant took a container of water and was able to pour the water into the jar. He had "filled" the jar four times.

He paused and asked the class, "Now what do we learn from this demonstration?" Immediately hands shot up, because the answer seemed too obvious. The class spokesman said, "Even when you think your schedule is full, there's always more you can add."

The consultant replied, "That's the obvious answer—and it's incorrect. The point of this demonstration is this: If you don't put the big rocks in first, they won't ever fit in later."

In life, you and I only have so many "big rocks" that we can fit into our lives. These represent our top priorities. If you don't make worship and rest one of your "big rocks," you never will experience God's best for your life.

The Sabbath commandment is not a MORAL LAW that we have to obey or we will be punished - it is a wonderful principle that you need to follow. If you refuse to follow it, you are only going to hurt yourself. God is saying, "Do yourself a favor. Set aside one day a week to worship and rest."

The Real Christian Sabbath Day
There is a final aspect of the Sabbath that we must examine. It has to do with our salvation. The Bible reveals it in Hebrews 4:9-11.

Substitute the word "sabbath" (the original Greek) for the word "rest" and read it aloud. Come on, read it out loud—you're not *that* busy.

> *"There remains, then, a Sabbath for the people of God; for anyone who enters God's <u>Sabbath</u> also <u>Sabbaths</u> from his own work, just as God did from His. Let us therefore, make every effort to enter that <u>Sabbath</u>, so that no one will fall by following their example of disobedience."*

This passage reveals that we do not have to **work** for our salvation. What is the opposite of rest? It's work. In the Old Testament, the Israelites had to work for their salvation by making sacrifices, keeping commandments, and performing a myriad of rituals, ceremonies, and rites. It was hard work to gain God's acceptance!

That's the beauty of salvation by grace. We don't have to work for salvation. Our salvation has already been provided; we simply rest in the finished work of Calvary. For us, Jesus worked for our salvation, so we can rest in His redemptive act.

How do you spell "salvation?" Some spell it "D-O." If you ask the average person on the street what it takes to go to heaven, they will start talking about all the things they have to DO. "This is what I do to go to heaven: go to church, give money, read my Bible, visit the sick, help the poor."

The New Testament spells salvation, "D-O-N-E." It's already done. God already provided salvation on the cross. In the Old Testament, the priests had to serve, and after they finished serving, they sat down and rested. That's exactly the opposite of what a New Testament Christian does. A New Testament Christian sits down and **rests** in the finished work of Jesus Christ, and then we rise up to **serve** God. We rest first, and then we serve. Because we are resting in the work of the cross, we don't have to work to earn our salvation. We give to the poor, help hurting people, visit the sick, give our money and read our Bibles because we LOVE JESUS, not to earn salvation. Jesus Christ gives us this rest—this Sabbath.

Come to Jesus and Rest!

One of the greatest invitations in the whole Bible is in Matthew 11:28. Jesus says, *"Come to me, all you who are weary and burdened, and I will give you rest."* He gives us the offer of rest for our souls. In a world that is so fast paced, where about all we've added is noise and speed, people are looking for rest. There is such a spirit of restlessness and Jesus says, "Come to me and I will give you inner rest for your soul."

Some say, "You mean I don't have to DO anything for my salvation? That sounds too easy." That seems un-American, because it is so contrary to the Protestant work ethic. We live among a generation who has earned their living by the sweat of their brow. You may earn a good living that way, but the only way you will gain salvation is by the blood of Jesus—not the sweat of your brow. You simply trust Jesus.

Let Go and Let God

There once was a man who was walking along a seaside cliff on a very dark night. He had walked along this path many times but did not know that a part of it had crumbled away. He stepped out into the open and found himself sliding down the edge of this cliff. He was frantically scratching and grabbing for anything to grasp to stop his fall, and finally he grabbed onto a small of a root that was hanging out of the face of the cliff. Hanging there, he could not see the stars above or the water below because the night was pitch black. The only sound he could hear was the crashing of the waves on the rocks below. Soon, his fingers grew tired and so he cried out, "God, please help me! Rescue me! Help me!"

In a few moments God said to the man, "Let go of the root and trust me."

"No, God! I can't do that. Can't you see I've got to hang on as tightly as I can?"

Again, he heard the voice, "Let go and trust me."

But he continues to hang on as long as he can. His arms begin to cramp. Sweat is dripping down his face. Finally, he says, "Okay, God. I'll let go and trust you. Here goes."

He released the root and fell...four inches onto a wide, rock path that was right below his feet all along. He felt like such a fool. He had been holding on for dear life when safety was just below his feet. Only when he let go of his own efforts did he learn that God could be trusted.

Many people still try to experience salvation by holding on to their own efforts, but salvation only comes by trusting God. That's the real meaning of the Sabbath, and it's the best application of the fourth commandment.

Every Day Is the Christian Sabbath Day
Therefore, if somebody asks you, "Is Sunday the Christian Sabbath?" you tell him or her, "Yes, Sunday is the Christian Sabbath." If somebody asks, "Is Monday the Christian Sabbath?" you say, "Yes, Monday is the Christian Sabbath." "Tuesday, Wednesday, Thursday, Friday, Saturday, Sunday?" Yes, that's correct. Every day that you have ceased from working for salvation and are resting in Jesus is the Sabbath day.

CHAPTER 5

What Are Your Family Values?

"Honor your father and your mother so that you may live long in the land the Lord your God is giving to you."

Exodus 20:12

One of the main reasons for the moral decline in America is that we have lost sight of what are often called "family values." Today, "family" doesn't even have the same meaning it did thirty years ago. Social scientists and some lawmakers are trying to redefine family to mean any group of people living together in any kind of relationship.

The first and best place to look for family values is in the Word of God. The fifth commandment is the pivotal commandment. The first four commandments address our vertical relationship with God. The last six commandments address our human (or horizontal) relationships. The arrangement of these commandments is not accidental or incidental; it is intentional. And the message is clear. We must be in a right relationship with God before we can relate correctly to those around us. As God shifts our attention toward human relations, the very first area that is addressed is the family.

A Word to Children

First, let's consider what this command is saying to children. What does it mean to "honor" your parents? The Hebrew word for "honor" is *kabed* which means, "to lend weight or dignity toward." Whether you are a child living at home or even an adult with one or more living parents, this command is still in force for you. We never grow out of the moral obligation that God has given us.

A Child's Focus: Obey Them

As you honor your parents, you pass through different phases of how you express honor to your parents. For instance, when you are a child, the focus should be on OBEDIENCE. In Ephesians 6:1, we read, *"Children, obey your parents in the Lord, for this is right."* Parents may not always *be* right, but it is right for a child to obey them. In the Bible, disobedience is a very serious crime.

Under the Law of Moses, if a child showed disrespect, dishonor, and disobedience to a parent, that child was to be brought outside the gates of the city and stoned to death (Deuteronomy 21:21). I wonder how many of us would be around today if we were stoned for disobeying our parents. Thank God, we are not under the law; we are under grace, but these verses let us know how seriously God regards disobedience.

What if parents are wrong? Obviously, when Scripture says we are to "obey them in the Lord" it means that His commands come first. This means that if a parent tells a child to do something contrary to His commands, such as murder, stealing, etc., the child is not obligated to obey. However, it's very rare for a parent to do that.

The Importance of Recognizing Authority

We are to obey our parents simply because God said to do it. God is preparing us for life because we spend our entire lives dealing with higher authorities. If we develop a habit of disrespect, rebellion and disobedience, there will be severe consequences down the road. If a child doesn't learn to submit to his or her parents, he or she won't find it easy to submit to teachers, bosses and even the police.

I have had the privilege of going into a number of state prisons to speak to the inmates. In talking to these prisoners, I have never heard one say, "This was my goal in life, to end up here—in prison." Not one of them wanted to end up in prison, but somewhere along the way, they got off track and started rebelling against authority. For many of them, they never learned the basics —to obey their parents. Because they were rebellious against their parents' authority, they became rebellious against school authority, then the law. The older we get, the more severe the consequences of disobedience.

The Bible teaches that those who don't learn to obey seldom live a long, happy life. This fifth commandment is the first one with a promise. The promise is simple: "Honor your parents, and you will live longer." Ephesians 6:2 explains this promise. *"Honor your father and mother—which is the first commandment with promise— that it may go well with you and that you may enjoy long life on the earth."* Notice that God says that you will ENJOY long life if you follow this commandment. I know a lot of old, miserable people. The best way to ensure that you enjoy a long and happy life is to OBEY your parents. God loves you so much that He tells you the secret to this kind of enjoyment.

A Teenager's Focus: Respect Them

As children grow into adolescence, the focus shifts to the need to show respect for their parents. During this time of growing, learning and changing, many teenagers think they know everything and can do everything. Teens look at parents, teachers, coaches and Sunday school teachers and say, "How could I have ever thought they were brilliant? They are brain dead." At this time of life, it is the natural response for teenagers to show disrespect and disdain for authority figures. However, a Christian teenager must resist this trend. The Bible clearly warns that if you don't show your parents respect, you will face serious consequences. Parents of teenagers should have this warning label attached to their foreheads: "WARNING: THE WORD OF GOD HAS DETERMINED THAT DISOBEDIENCE AND DISRESPECT TO YOUR PARENTS CAN BE HARMFUL TO YOUR HEALTH AND WELL BEING."

It's tough to raise teenagers. Mark Twain used to say, "When your son turns 13, put him in a barrel, and feed him through the knot hole. When he turns 16, plug up the knot hole!" Sure it's tough to raise teenagers—because it is tough to BE a teenager.

Teenagers often become sullen because they are certain that their parents don't have a clue about what it means to be a teenager. They often forget the obvious truth that every parent was a teenager at one time. The times may be different, but the hormones and the pressures are exactly the same. Are today's teenagers much different than previous generations? Each generation comes up with song lyrics that are totally meaningless. When my girls were teenagers, they listened to by a group called The Dead Presidents. This group sang deep, profound lyrics like "Going to the country, gonna get me a bunch of peaches, going to the country, gonna eat me a lot of peaches, going to the country, gonna . . ." Teenagers think that is so cool and can't imagine that their parents ever listened to songs like that.

Well, my generation had meaningless lyrics, too. When I was a teenager, we listened to deep truths like, "Wild thing, you make my heart sing. You make everything groovy." How profound. The Beatles sang, "He come on flat-top. He come groovin' up slowly. He got ju-ju eyeballs, he one holy roller, he got feet down below his knees, got to be a joker 'cause he's so hard to please." Hello? Does anyone have a clue about what that song is saying?

Even a generation before mine had their share of silly lyrics. They listened to songs like this, "I want to be kissed by you—by you—and nobody else but you, de doo doop de doo." Teenagers of every generation have shared the same thoughts, feelings and problems that the current generation of teenagers are feeling.

If teenagers can just realize this and keep respecting their parents until they "survive" adolescence, God will bless the rest of their life. Sadly, too many teenagers lose respect for their parents, and it leads to all kinds of ruin and destruction.

How to Reform Your Parents

If you happen to be a teenager reading this book (or if your parents tell you to read this chapter), you may be wondering how you can change your parents so that your life will be more tolerable. Here's some sure-fire parent-reforming strategies:

    (1) Try courtesy and good manners. Add these eight

simple phrases to your vocabulary: "Yes sir; Yes ma'am; Thank you; I'm sorry." You will find that when you use good manners, your parents will be shocked at first, but then they will start treating you with more respect, too. Before long, you will find that they are getting smarter and easier to get along with.

(2) Try expressing appreciation to them. Fast-forward your life about 20 years until you have kids. Imagine how good it will make you feel when your kids tell you how much they appreciate you. Since you will want your kids to love and appreciate you, remember that what you sow in life you are going to reap. The only way to reap a crop of appreciation from your future children is to plant plenty of seeds of appreciation with your parents today.

A teenager went to see a psychiatrist because he was stressed out. The psychiatrist said, "Tell me about your family life."

The teenager said, "Well, my dad loves me and buys me things. He takes me to ball games, and we fish and hunt together. We are real buddies. We do lots of things together. My mom cooks for me. She cleans my clothes and tells me she loves me. She hugs me regularly and tells me that she is proud of me."

The psychiatrist was puzzled. He said, "It sounds like you have a great family life. Why are you so stressed out?"

The kid said, "I'm afraid they are going to escape."

Most teenagers have a good life at home. So, try telling your folks, "Thank you. I appreciate you." You will be pleasantly surprised by their reaction.

(3) Try helpfulness. If you are a teenager reading this, let me ask you, "What does your bedroom look like right now?" The city dump? I heard about a kid who was looking at his parents' wedding pictures and asked his dad, "Is this when Mom came to work for us?" Teenagers, let me give you a hint. Your parents don't exist to pick up after you. As a part of the family, you need to help them keep things neat. Here's a practical assignment: First, clean up your room without being asked, then go to your mom and ask if there is anything else you can do to help her around the house today. (You had better know how to perform CPR.)

These little suggestions will make your teenage years a lot more bearable. You will be making an investment in respect that will pay big dividends in your future. Take good care of your parents—they are the only ones you will ever have.

The Adult Child's Focus: Treasure Them

Even when we become adults, we are still bound by the fifth commandment. We are no longer are obligated to obey them, but we are always to honor them. This means that when you and your parents grow older, you are to treasure your parents. As parents grow older, they often become dependent on their grown children. Don't see them as a burden but as a blessing. After all, they cared for us when we were totally dependent on them. There are several ways that grown children may honor their parents.

It is very important that you provide for them financially. The Bible gives a harsh warning in I Timothy 5:8, *"If anyone does not provide for his relatives, and especially for his immediate family, he has denied the faith and is worse than an unbeliever."* It's hard to imagine anything worse than being an unbeliever, but the Bible says that if a person claims to be a Christian and doesn't care for his or her family members, he or she is worse than an unbeliever is. That's how strongly God upholds this fifth commandment.

Treasuring your aging parents means more than just celebrating their 50th wedding anniversary. It means more than sending them an occasional card or paying for them to live in a nursing home. It means that as they get older, you continue to treat them with dignity, treasure your relationship with them and communicate your love to them.

Should We Just Get Rid of the Elderly?

Throughout history, the most wicked civilizations have always neglected the elderly. In the Roman Empire, as late as 60 AD, they were still taking old people and drowning them in the Tiber River. Some are advocating today that when people reach an advanced age, they are worthless to society. To some, old people are seen as an inconvenience and a drain on our resources.

One of the scariest things about America's moral decay is that we have come to de-value life. For the sake of "convenience" we have killed 40 million unborn babies since legalizing abortion in

1973. The next logical step in this "disposable-life" mindset is to encourage euthanasia for the elderly (ever heard of Dr. Kevorkian?) The next step after that is mandatory elimination of those who no longer contribute to society. After all, the secular humanists have been teaching us that "only the strong survive."

Technology is advancing and medical science is developing to the point where people are living longer and longer. Many people who are 60 and 70 years old are still dealing with their living parents. Regardless of the age or health of your parents, God's Word says that you must *always* honor and respect them. You are bound by this commandment until they die.

A pastor friend of mine told this story about a family he knew. This family had built a beautiful new home and the wife was very proud of her new dwelling. She was almost fanatical about keeping it clean. Not long after they moved into the new home, the husband's elderly father came to live with them. The old gentleman was suffering from a form of palsy and could hardly lift a fork of food to his mouth without a spill.

The wife became so angry with the constant mess that she directed her husband to build a wooden tray for his father to use when he ate. It looked like a small feeding trough. Eating in this feeding trough robbed the old man of the little dignity he still possessed. But at least the kitchen was staying clean.

One day, when the wife was walking beside the workshop, she stopped when she heard her twelve-year-old son hammering. She asked, "Honey, what are you building?" He said, "I am building a feed trough for you, for when you get old." The woman realized the terrible shame of the feeding trough, and she never again required him to eat from it.

People do many unkind things to rob the dignity of those who have reached an advanced age. The Bible says that wisdom, experience and gray hair are crowns of wisdom. We should afford more honor and respect to those who are old.

What If My Parents Aren't Honorable?

You may have a problem with honoring your parents because you have parents who haven't treated you in ways that are honorable.

Perhaps you have been the victim of verbal, physical or sexual abuse. Maybe you are angry with your mom or dad because they divorced, mistreated you or failed to show the kind of love you think you deserved. Maybe you feel they were too strict, or maybe they never hugged you and said they loved you. Even though you are now an adult, you may still be harboring resentment and bitterness toward them. How can you honor them if this is the case? First, admit there is a problem. If possible, in a loving way, communicate those feelings to your parents. Don't let another week go without addressing the issue. Express your frustrations and feelings with them. Then, forgive your parents and ask them to forgive you for not treasuring them the way you should. The last years of your relationship can be the best.

I've counseled many adults who find it hard to honor their parents. On many occasions, I've stood beside an open casket and heard adult children weeping in agony. These tears are sometimes not so much out of remorse of the death of that parent but out of a sense of guilt because they did not truly treasure, cherish and value their parent in his or her last years of life. Don't be guilty of that. Don't wait until it's too late to begin to treasure them. Love, treasure and cherish your parents now. Remember, dead noses smell no roses. An expensive casket or an ornate spray of flowers won't have any impact on them once they're gone. A single conversation that addresses your feelings is the only way to resolve this problem.

The Focus of Parents: Be Honorable

Hidden below the surface of the fifth commandment is a principle for parents. Your responsibility is that you must *be honorable* and strive to be the kind of parent that your children can honor. The very best thing that parents can give their children is A GOOD EXAMPLE of what is right and what is wrong.

I've heard some parents say, "I don't want to plant any moral or religious thoughts in their mind. I want them to grow up and choose for themselves what they want to believe."

That is very dangerous attitude. That would be like a farmer going out to his empty field and saying to the dirt, "Dirt, what do you want to be? If you want to be zucchini, be zucchini. If you want to be tomatoes, be tomatoes. If you want to be corn, be corn. Be anything you want to be, and don't let me influence you." That farmer is going to harvest a crop of weeds because farming is deliberate. A farmer must cultivate and care for a crop in order to produce worthwhile results.

If you, as a parent, have that hands-off attitude, you will harvest a bitter crop of moral, ethical and spiritual weeds. Television, music and peers are teaching our children the ways of the world; so wise, honorable parents must give their children a personal example of God's standards.

One of the best lessons we can teach our children is that there are rules to follow, and that sure and swift punishment will follow if those rules are broken. That's precisely what God is saying in the Ten Commandments.

Sadly, we have lived through a time when the social scientists are telling us that children shouldn't be threatened or punished. An entire generation of parents swallowed the permissive philosophy of Dr. Spock, who taught that if Junior wanted to cut the leg off your dining room table, don't stop him, or punish him. Just make sure the saw is sharp so he won't be frustrated. We are now reaping the harvest of this kind of parenting.

Paul Harvey relates a story about parenting that happened in a crowded department store one Christmas. A five-year-old boy is sitting on a spring loaded rocking horses that had a sign "Display only. Do not touch." He is gleefully rocking back and forth. His mother is standing there ringing her hands saying, "Please, Junior, get off that rocking horse." Junior ignores her and keeps on rocking.

One of the store's Santas walks by. Immediately he understands what is going on, bends down and whispers something in the ear of that little boy. The little boy immediately gets off the horse and stands next to his mother.

The mother says, "Oh, thank you Santa. That was so wonderful. What did you promise you would bring little Junior if he would get off that horse?"

The tired Santa looked at her with a steady eye and said, "Lady, I said:, 'You little brat, if you don't get off that horse, I'm going to put you over my knee and spank you.'"

Our children are going to grow up and treat their children the way we treat them. That's why an honorable parent sets a good example. Paul said in 1 Corinthians 11:1, *"Follow my example, as I follow the example of Christ."* We must realize that children are going to follow our example before they follow our teaching.

The phone rang in one home and the young mother instructed her daughter to tell the caller that she wasn't at home. The little girl said to the caller, "My mother told me to tell you that she is not here." That day, the mother realized the error of her way.

Parents, you can tell your kids to pray, but unless they see that prayer is important to you, chances are they are not going to pray much. You can tell them to read the Bible, but unless they observe you studying the Word, they are not going to read it much. We can tell our kids the importance of going to church and worshiping, but if they see our inconsistency when it rains or when we are tired from a Saturday night party, that will speak much louder than any words we can ever speak.

Vance Havner tells the story about a lady in a Southern town who had one daughter, whom she intended to raise as a real Southern lady. She taught her how to dress, how to put on makeup and how to fix her hair. She instructed her on how to enter a room, how to stand and how to sit. She entered her in all the beauty pageants and made sure she was first in line for the debutante ball.

When the daughter was a teenager, she was involved in an automobile accident, and her mother rushed to the intensive care unit to find her precious daughter near the point of death. The daughter said to her mom, "Mother, you taught me to fix my hair and put on makeup. You taught me how to hold a cigarette. You taught me how to hold a cocktail. But Mother, I'm scared because you never taught me how to be ready to die."

Parents, in teaching your children everything else in life, do not neglect to teach them the great spiritual truths of life. Teach them how to get ready to meet God. Teach them that each person must enter into a personal relationship with God through Jesus Christ. The most honorable thing you can do is to make it a privilege and a joy for your children to honor you as God requires them to do.

CHAPTER 6

God Is Pro-Life

"You shall not murder."
Exodus 20:13

Y ou may feel confident considering commandments six and seven because you may be thinking that you haven't killed anyone or committed adultery. However, Lord Jesus Christ expanded this commandment to include more than just physical murder or physical adultery. Jesus spoke of the DESIRE to kill or to commit adultery as being sin as well. By the time we have completed this chapter, the Holy Spirit of God may reveal to you that while you have not committed homicide (shedding of blood), you may be guilty of intent-to-murder by committing "angercide."

Is All Killing a Sin?
Some people believe that this commandment forbids killing of any kind. They believe that it is wrong to kill a bug, or a deer, or a fish, or an enemy soldier. The King James Version reads, *"Thou shalt not kill."* The word for "kill" is the Hebrew word *rotsock* which literally means "to murder." That's a better translation than the general word "kill," which has created much confusion. There are several kinds of killing that are excluded from this command.

For instance, hunting and fishing are excluded from this law. God said in Genesis 9:3, *"Everything that lives and moves will be food for you. Just as I gave you the green plants, I now give you everything."* Obviously, God was allowing the killing of animals for food. While the Bible does not prohibit this kind of hunting or fishing, it is certainly wrong to indiscriminately kill animals for the "thrill of the hunt."

Albert Schweitzer, the renowned missionary doctor, taught that the sixth commandment forbade killing any kinds of animals. When he was in Africa, he would never even kill a mosquito because he thought that was breaking the sixth commandment. It's rather ironic to realize that when the doctor poured disinfectant on a wound, he was killing thousands of microscopic germs.

Another debate rages about whether capital punishment is allowed in the Bible. When you study the totality of Scripture, you will see that this commandment does not prohibit capital punishment. Romans 13:1–5 tells us that we should submit to the governmental authorities over us. We should submit ourselves to our civil law—to the police, the courts and the criminal justice system of our land. Paul makes a great argument for that in the first few verses of Romans 13. He says that God has ordained those authorities, even the secular authorities, and has positioned them there.

> *"For rulers hold no terror for those who do right, but for those who do wrong. Do you want to be free from fear of the one in authority? Then do what is right and he will commend you. For he is God's servant to do you good. But if you do wrong, be afraid, for he does not bear the sword for nothing. He is God's servant, an agent of wrath to bring punishment on the wrongdoer. Therefore, it is necessary to submit to the authorities, not only because of possible punishment but also because of conscience."*
>
> Romans 13:3–5

Paul uses the phrase "the power of the sword," which means that God has given government and its criminal justice system the authority to impose capital punishment. A sword, especially in Bible times, was used to behead the worst criminals. A sword was never used to spank or to injure people—it was used to execute them. Paul could have used the phrase "the power of the whip," but he chose to use "sword" which promotes the justification of capital punishment.

What about self-defense? If someone broke into my house and threatened my family, would I violate this commandment if I defended myself and my family? Elsewhere in the book of Exodus, it is very clear that we have a right to defend ourselves, and if we kill someone while defending ourselves, we are not violating this law (see Exodus 21:12; 22:2).

The Quakers are known as a peace-loving people. They believe in hunting, but they would never kill a person for any reason. They teach that if someone attacks and kills them, there is really nothing they can do because they cannot kill in self-defense. I heard a humorous story about a Quaker gentleman who was asleep one night and heard an intruder in his home. He went downstairs and pointed his old shotgun at the robber and said, "The Bible says 'Thou shall not kill,' but I want to inform thee that thou art standing between me and a deer I am about to shoot." There always seems to be a loophole!

In addition, killing as part of a national war is not prohibited in this commandment. Jesus said that there would always be wars and rumors of wars (Matt. 24:6). This is just an unfortunate reality of mankind's sinfulness. Someone has said that "war is hell," but that's not true. War is not hell; only hell is hell. To say, "War is hell" is to say, "Peace is heaven." Hell is a lot worse than war can ever be. In the Bible there are dozens of occasions when God instructed His people to go into battle. War is corporate self-defense and there are times when nations must go to war.

During World War II, some citizens of Germany considered themselves pacifists. One was a Lutheran preacher, Dietrich Bonhoeffer, author of *The Cost of Discipleship.* [iii] As Adolph Hitler systematically attempted to execute an entire race of people, Bonhoeffer and a group of Lutheran pastors soon reversed their pacifist stance. They were so alarmed by the Nazi movement that they even devised a plot to assassinate Adolph Hitler. They came to consider him as Satan incarnate. Tragically, the Nazis discovered their plot and executed them in a German prison. It has been said that in the Nazi prison camps there were no pacifists. As tragic as it may be, there are times when a nation and a people must gather together in war, and lives are lost in this process.

Homicide Is Prohibited

Intentional murder is what that word *rotsock* forbids. This refers to one individual taking the life of another because of personal anger or hostility toward that person. This kind of murder can be expressed in different ways. First, there is what we often call **homicide**—a general word for killing another person. The pages of the Bible are covered with the blood of murders. In Genesis 4:8, we are told that Cain killed his brother, Abel, thus becoming the first murderer. The moment he took the life of his brother, he knew he had done something that was unacceptable (even though the sixth commandment hadn't been given yet). He didn't want to answer God truthfully when asked about his fatal deed. Moses murdered an Egyptian when a lesser punishment was appropriate. When David arranged for the death of Uriah the Hittite, he was just as guilty as if he had plunged the spear into his body himself.

By the way, it's helpful to compare and contrast the killing that took place at the scene where Uriah was murdered. The Bible never hints that the soldiers were committing murder—they were fighting for their respective nations. The weren't breaking this commandment. However, because David arranged the death of Uriah out of a personal motive, he broke this command (see 2 Samuel 11).

Another symptom of America's moral decay is the prevalence of violence and murder. America leads the civilized world in our level of violence. Some Europeans have expressed to me that they are afraid to visit America because of the widespread threat of violence. Someone is murdered in America every eight minutes. While you are reading this chapter, four Americans will become the victim of homicide. Jesus taught that the anger and hatred that motivates murder comes from a sinful heart. He said, *"For from within, out of men's hearts, come evil thoughts, sexual immorality, theft, murder, adultery"* (Mark 7:21).

Suicide Is Prohibited

Suicide is just self-homicide, and it violates this commandment. What does the Bible say about suicide? The main teaching is found here in Exodus 20:13. which simply says, *"You shall not murder."* A person who commits suicide is assuming the role of God. This person snatches God's timetable into his or her own hands. The Bible says, *"Man is destined to die once, and after that to face judgment"* (Hebrews 9:27). God has already determined when a person will die—suicide abrogates God's plan. Taking your own life is as much a sin as taking someone else's life.

People often ask me if a person who commits suicide goes to heaven. It all depends—is that person truly saved? I believe that, on rare occasions, there are some Christians who have become so depressed, despondent and discouraged that they have committed suicide. Did they go to heaven? Absolutely. Some who are not Christians have committed suicide. Did they go to heaven? No.

You see, there is only one unforgivable sin. It is not the sin of suicide. The only unforgivable sin Jesus identified is blasphemy against the Holy Spirit—-final and complete unbelief. He said, *"All the sins and blasphemies of men will be forgiven them. But whoever blasphemes against the Holy spirit will never be forgiven; he is guilty of an eternal sin"* (Mark 3:28–29). To blaspheme means to "speak against." This sin is committed when a person speaks a final and ultimate "No" to the conviction of the Holy Spirit.

In contrast, the Catholic Church teaches, as part of their official dogma, that suicide is a mortal sin for which there is no forgiveness. They teach that every person who commits suicide goes to hell. However, I respectfully disagree with their position. I believe the Bible teaches that when a person becomes a Christian, Jesus **forgives** every sin that person has ever committed—and every sin they will ever commit. A Christian is under the cleansing blood of Jesus Christ, and the penalty of sin is removed.

However, I must add that any Christian who commits suicide will stand before Jesus with a tremendous sense of regret and remorse. The Lord Jesus will be extremely displeased with the choice they made. These Christians will lose every reward that was coming to them, and I think they will be heartbroken over that decision they made.

In America, suicide constitutes the second most common way that teenagers die. Every 21 minutes in America, a teenager commits suicide. Sometimes teenagers get discouraged and think the best way out of all their pain is to "end it all." The terrible fallacy of this idea is that suicide **doesn't** end it. The only thing suicide ends is the beating of a heart. There is always something after death. Suicide doesn't end it for the victim. Neither does it end it for the family members and friends who are left behind to grieve in an especially painful way. The main thing suicide ends is the potential for that person to enjoy the rest of his or her life.

Perhaps you are reading this, and you are contemplating suicide. You may feel that you have reached the point where life seems unbearably bad—and you can't see any hope of it getting any better. If you feel this way, I encourage you to talk to someone—a family member, a member of your church or a professional counselor. There are people who want to help you pass through this time of discouragement.

You would be violating God's wonderful plan for your life if you ever attempt suicide. Sure, life gets tough for all of us. However, just remember that God loves you, and He promised you in 1 Corinthians 10:13, *"No temptation has seized you except what is common to man. And God is faithful; he will not let you be tempted beyond what you can bear. But when you are tempted, he will also provide a way out so that you can stand up under it."* Everybody faces temptation. Don't give in to the temptation to commit suicide, and don't give up on God!

Infanticide Is Murder

The third way this commandment can be violated is by infanticide—the killing of infants. This includes both the killing of a newborn infant or a pre-born infant. I sincerely believe abortion is America's worst violation of the sixth commandment. How has our culture become so insensitive to the value of life that we can sanction the medical removal of a child from its mother's womb?

Remember, every eight minutes there is a murder; every twenty-one minutes there is a suicide by a teenager. Those statistics may alarm you, but it is unthinkable that every 21 **seconds** in America a life is snuffed out. The debate continues to rage about when "life" begins. But no one can deny that abortion stops a beating heart. I read a profound statement on a bumper sticker not long ago that said, "Of all the patients that go into an abortion clinic only half of them leave alive."

"A couple of years ago a teenager, Maria, 28 weeks pregnant, went into a Pine Bluff, Arkansas abortion clinic. A friend accompanied her. When the fetus was delivered, the child was alive. The abortion doctor took the child, put it into a paper sack, wrapped it up and placed it on the table to the side. Maria's friend was enraged. She immediately picked up the newborn baby and took it to the emergency room of a hospital. The doctors began to try to preserve the life of this two-pound baby. After several weeks and $300,000 of medical care, the young girl is expected to live." [iv]

What would have happened if the friend had not been there to say, "I think this life is worth saving"?

On January 22, 1973, at the conclusion of the Roe vs. Wade lawsuit, nine black-robed men in America issued this landmark decree: *"The states may not prohibit abortions at any time if the life or health of the mother is at stake."* Since that ruling, lower courts have interpreted the phrase "health of the mother" to mean not only **physical** health, but also emotional, mental, or even economic health. This means that if a pregnant woman claims that her unborn child will cause her stress or economic hardship—she is legally entitled to an abortion—often paid for by our tax dollars.

President Bush signed a new law into effect in 2003 prohibiting late-term abortions in the United States. The facts on late-term abortion are staggering. In 1996 in the state of New York , 4000 third-trimester babies were aborted. (Any honest doctor would admit that ALL of these babies had a chance to live outside the womb.) If there had been an earthquake, hurricane, tornado or other natural disaster in which 4000 people had died, it would have been the leading news item for months. Yet abortion is the "silent disaster" that is so easy to ignore.

We are horrified by the millions of Jews who were put to death during the Holocaust of World War II. In the last two decades, however, America has conducted its own silent holocaust by murdering millions of these innocent lives.

Some claim that abortion should be allowed in the case of rape and incest. As tragic as that is, we must carefully consider the consequences of this position. For example, consider the story of the gospel singer, Ethel Waters, who was conceived as the result of rape. We can all thank God that Ethel Waters was not aborted. She has been an inspiration to millions as she sang "His Eye is on the Sparrow" and "God Don't Make No Junk."

Incest is unspeakably wicked. However, did you know that Ruth, who was an ancestress of the Lord Jesus born in the family of Moab, was born as the result of an incestuous relationship? That family in which incest occurred is part of the genealogy of the Lord Jesus Christ. As terrible as it is, I contend that we must allow God to determine the outcome of such tragedies. After all, He is the One who knows the person even in the womb. He says to Jeremiah in Jeremiah 1:5, *"I knew you before I formed you in the womb."* To me, that's all the scripture needed to settle the ethical issue of when life begins. When Mary was pregnant with the Lord Jesus Christ, she went to see her cousin Elizabeth. Elizabeth's unborn child, John the Baptist, leaped with joy. That speaks volumes about the viability of life in the womb.

Abortion Sheds Innocent Blood

Proverbs 6:16 outlines seven things that God hates. Included on the list are *"hands that shed innocent blood"* (Proverbs 6:17). If someone attacks you, you will try to defend yourself. If someone threatens someone you love, you will try to defend him or her as well. How tragic that these pre-born babies, who are so innocent, can't defend themselves against the abortionist. There are so few people who are fighting for the rights of these tiny Americans.

Dr. Bernard Lagune, a distinguished obstetrician wrote, "If a mother's life is in danger, I never attack the child. I try to save the life of the mother, and then if the child dies in the process, so be it." There are cases when a complication in pregnancy threatens the mother's life. In such situations, a wise doctor will try to save the mother's life, and, if possible, the life of the child.

Abortion-on-demand is just another sign that America is sinking deeper into the pit of moral slime. Each abortion reduces the national value of human life. The Roman leader, Seneca, wrote about a barbaric custom in the Roman Empire: "Mad dogs we knock on the head; fierce and savage oxen we slay; sickly sheep we put to the knife to keep them from infecting the flock; unnatural babies we destroy. We drown even children who at birth are weak and abnormal." This sounds like America at the end of the 20th Century.

Should abnormal babies be aborted? Who is the person qualified to determine who is "normal" and who is not? None of us is perfect. The moment we start indiscriminately killing deformed pre-born children, it is a short step away to exterminating those who are born with some kind of deformity or develop some handicap in life.

What about the argument, "It's a woman's body. Shouldn't she have the right to do with it what she wants to do?" Abortion proponents are quick to shout about how a woman should have a CHOICE. I firmly agree. However, that control and choice should be wisely exercised at the time of the sexual encounter. When a life has been created, God has stepped into the picture. Of course, it's her own body, but a baby is not simply a part of her; it is a person. Our society protects people from hurting themselves, doesn't it?

I could say to you, "It's my body, I can do anything with my body I want to." I could say it, but I hope you would not respect that statement if I took a hatchet and began to chop off my fingers, one by one. I hope someone would wrestle that hatchet away from me. We need to show the same kind of concern for the unborn as well.

It's Not My Problem

You may be thinking, "I've never had an abortion. In fact, I don't even know anyone who has had an abortion, so this issue doesn't pertain to me." If you are a Christian, you can't ignore it. If you are a conscientious American, you must see this issue as one of the leading reasons that we are choking in a toxic moral vapor. As concerned Christians, we should stand up and say clearly, "On the basis of my Christian conviction, I think abortion is murder."

Dante wrote in *The Inferno,* "The hottest place in hell is reserved for those, who in a time of moral crisis, remain silent." [v] In

America, we are facing a moral crisis. Silence is not golden; in this case, silence is yellow—cowardly. We need to realize abortion is a violation of the sixth commandment.

Beware of "Invisible Murder"

Homicide, suicide and abortion are examples of what may be called INTENTIONAL murder. The sixth commandment may also be violated by something that can be called INVISIBLE murder. In this case, there is no smoking gun or bloody knife—there isn't even a funeral. Instead, it consists of the kind of hatred directed toward a person that wishes that person were dead. We read in 1 John 3:15, *"Anyone who hates his brother is a murderer, and you know that no murderer has eternal life in him."* Jesus confirmed his commentary on the sixth commandment:

> *"You have heard that it was said to the people long ago, 'Do not murder, and anyone who murders will be subject to judgment.' But I tell you that anyone who is angry with his brother will be subject to judgment. Again, anyone who says to his brother, 'Raca,'* (which means you empty-headed fool) *is answerable to the Sanhedrin. But anyone who says, 'You fool!'* (which means morally corrupt) *will be in danger of the fire of hell."*
>
> Matthew 5:21

Jesus is pointing out that while you may not be guilty of homicide, it's possible that you have committed murder by "angercide." We've all heard the expression, "If looks could kill..." Have you ever had hateful thoughts about somebody and wished they would suffer? You may not be the one to do something harmful to them, but you would be secretly pleased if something unpleasant happened to them. When you bear this kind of attitude toward someone, you are guilty of violating the sixth commandment, according to the Lord Jesus Christ.

When I was a child, I heard the expression, "Sticks and stones may break my bones, but words will never hurt me." That is a lie.

Angry words can often inflict more pain than sticks and stones—words can break hearts and hopes. Angry words can even break up homes. When you use angry words as offensive weapons against your spouse, children and coworkers, you may be violating the sixth commandment.

Life Is Too Short to Carry a Grudge!

As we have seen to be true of the previous commandments, this prohibition has a positive side as well. The positive expression of this law is that we must value and cherish life—both our life and the lives of others. Life is a precious commodity. That is why the Psalmist says in Psalm 90:12, *"Teach us to number our days."* Each day of life is a precious gift from God. If I asked you how old you are, you would probably answer in years. While we generally count our age in years, the Bible say we should number each day of our life. If you want to do this, just multiply your years times 365 then factor in leap years. (One leap year every four years) Then add how many days since your last birthday and you will know exactly how many days you have lived. When you begin to value life as a precious commodity, you won't have a desire to hurt others.

Be willing to forgive others quickly so that your heart won't be full of bitterness or resentment. Unforgiveness is an acid that only destroys its own container. Your willingness to forgive others is proof that YOU HAVE BEEN forgiven by Jesus. He said in Mark 11:26, *"The same way you forgive the sins of others is the way your Father is going to forgive you."* God is going to hold us accountable for the way we forgive others.

Perhaps you've heard of Corrie ten Boom. During World War II, Corrie and her sister, Betsy, were arrested and taken to a concentration camp because their family harbored Jews during the Nazi takeover of Poland and the Netherlands. If you have read her book, *The Hiding Place*, you know about the terrible atrocities they endured in this camp.[vi] They had no privacy or respect, and the Nazis forced them to work in cruel conditions. Betsy died in the concentration camp, but Corrie survived. For years after this terrible experience, Corrie spoke to church groups about how God's grace sustained her through these trials.

Several years after the war, she was speaking in a church in the southern part of Germany. After the service, a large man came up to her and extended his hand toward her. She recognized him immediately. He was one of the cruelest guards in the concentration camp. Corrie was filled with repulsion as she remembered that he was the one who had brutally mistreated others. He asked if she recognized him, and she nodded wordlessly.

As he held out his hand, the former guard said in a thick accent, "I, too, am now a believer in Jesus Christ, and I have come to ask you to forgive me."

All the misery and animosity of the prison camp flooded her mind. She could not lift her hand to take his. As she looked into the face of that man, the only emotion she felt was anger and hatred. In a split second of grace, a realization came flooding into her heart. She realized that God had forgiven him and God loved him.

She prayed a silent prayer, "Jesus, I cannot love and forgive him, but You can love him through me and You can forgive him through me." She writes that it was as if a warm current of electricity was flowing through her as she felt her arm reaching up and her hand reaching out to take the hand of that prison guard. She looked him in the eye and said, "Brother, Jesus in me loves you and Jesus in me forgives you." She pulled him close and found through Jesus she was putting her arms around him.

Obeying the sixth commandment means more than merely refraining from murder. To honor God, you must make sure your heart stays clean from the evil thoughts and attitudes of anger and bitterness. You say that there is someone that you just CAN'T forgive. Maybe not, but Jesus in you can forgive that person ... if you will let Him.

CHAPTER 7

"The Myth of the Greener Grass"

"You shall not commit adultery."
Exodus 20:14

You might read that and think, "Well, I am safe there." Don't be too quick to ignore this because in Matthew 5:27, Jesus Christ said, *"You have heard that it was said, `Do not commit adultery' but I tell you that anyone who looks at a woman lustfully has already committed adultery with her in his heart."*

America is slipping deeper into a moral chasm because thousands of husbands and wives have ignored this command. It seems that people are looking for a new sexual thrill that they are certain can't be found in their marriage. In speaking of adultery, someone has claimed, "The grass is always greener on the other side of the fence." Well, it may be greener, but, trust me, you can't afford the water bill!

I heard about a little farm boy who came home from Sunday school after his class had been studying the Ten Commandments. He wasn't quite sure about the seventh commandment and asked his father, "Daddy, what did God mean when he said, `Thou shalt not commit *agriculture*?'" Instead of laughing at his mistake, his wise father didn't bat an eye and said, "Son, that means that you are not supposed to plow your neighbor's field." There is a lot of truth in that.

W.C. Fields, the noted comedian, was known as an irreligious and promiscuous person. One day he was found in his dressing room reading a Bible. His friend who caught him reading the Bible asked him, "W.C., what are you doing reading the Bible? I didn't think you believed any of that."

W.C. Fields closed the book and reportedly said, "Just looking for loopholes."

When it comes to the seventh commandment, there are no loopholes. Adultery has broken up marriages, ruined careers, and caused general misery for centuries. God loves you so much that He wants you to avoid the suffering that comes with breaking this commandment. There is a great deal of misunderstanding about sexual sin. Let's look at three questions related to this commandment.

What Is Adultery?

Simply stated, adultery is any sex outside the marriage relationship. If you aren't married, you may be thinking, "I can't violate the seventh commandment because I am single." The Hebrew word for adultery is *na-aph* which simply means "sexual sin" outside of marriage. If you are single, pre-marital sex violates this command. If you are married, you can violate the seventh commandment with extramarital sex. Any sexual behavior outside the bonds of marriage is a violation of the seventh commandment.

Adultery has destroyed thousands of marriages. Here's the typical American scenario: Jim and Mary meet in high school or college, and they get married. At the start, there is a lot of sizzle in their relationship. They start a family, and work hard at building their careers. After about six or seven years, the excitement level has lost some of its sizzle, and they no longer feel the same electricity that they once did, but they have grown comfortable in their relationship.

One day, a young girl starts working in Jim's office, and he begins to get to know her. He notices that she is always dressed nicely, and her hair is always fixed. Every day she looks like the cover of *Glamour* magazine, and he begins to compare her to his wife. Of course, he sees his wife early in the morning and late at night when she may not look her best. He begins to discuss business deals with this girl in his office, and she listens and really seems to care about what he is feeling. He thinks about his wife who sometimes criticizes him about things she doesn't like. Soon, he begins to compare the two women more and more.

Before long, he starts scheduling business lunches with her, and he finds that he enjoys her company. It seems harmless—after all it's just business. Soon, they find themselves alone in the office working late and the next step to adultery is fairly easy. But hey, she makes him feel young again! Soon, they are meeting on a regular basis, and he is torn between the guilt he feels about his wife and the sizzle he feels with his mistress. What started out to be pleasure soon turns into a prison from which they cannot escape. That's just a typical scenario, and you would be amazed at how many times it happens in America.

Adultery can also be committed through sexual fantasy. Even if you have never been physically involved outside your marriage, Jesus said you can violate this commandment in your mind and in your heart if you fantasize about a sexual relationship with someone who is not your spouse. It may be someone you know personally or a total stranger. Is it wrong to look at another person and think that he or she is attractive? No, that's normal. However, if you allow your look to linger, and then begin to mentally undress and fantasize about that person, you have just stepped over the line into "mental adultery."

Someone has said, "You can't keep the birds from flying over your head, but you can keep them from building a nest in your hair." The same is true about tempting thoughts. To have a tempting thought is not sin—but to entertain that thought is to cross over into sin. The first look at an attractive person usually is not sin, but it is the second, third, and fourth look can become sin. Sexual fantasy often leads to sexual sin. It is only a short step on a slippery slope to graduate from fantasizing about somebody to enacting that fantasy.

One of the greatest romantic tragedies of history is described in the story of *Camelot.* King Arthur and his wife, Guinevere, were deeply in love. The peacefulness and stability of their marriage was characteristic of Arthur's kingdom. In fact, the fidelity in their relationship was a model for the faithful integrity of the Knights of the Round Table.

Then Lancelot enters the picture. What began as a harmless look soon became a thought, and the thought became a touch, and the touch became a kiss, and the kiss became adultery. Ultimately, disaster descended upon the entire kingdom. Lives were ruined, homes were wrecked, and marriages were destroyed. However, it all started with what may have seemed like a harmless thought, a fantasy.

Why Is Adultery Such a Problem?

Is adultery a problem in America? The Hite Study of American Sexuality revealed the shocking statistic that 66% of American married men have been involved in extramarital relationships.[vii] Forty-nine percent of American women surveyed admitted that they had been involved in a sexual relationship outside their marriage. That number of adulterous men has been holding steady for the past three decades. However, there has been an alarming increase for women. Thirty years ago, only 25% of women were unfaithful to their husbands.

It's interesting to note that the statistics are about the same for single people. About 7 out of 10 single men over the age of 18 and about 5 out of 10 unmarried women over the age of 18 claimed to be sexually active.

Why is adultery such a problem in America that it is threatening our survival as a nation? First, we have to understand that God has created each of us with a powerful sex drive. Sex was not something that we dreamed up; it is a gift from God. In our society, we often consider sex as something vulgar, but in God's eyes, sex between a husband and wife is holy and pure. God created sex to enable people to express intimate affection between a man and a woman in marriage. Your sex drive is not something that should make you feel ashamed—it should be enjoyed—but ONLY in the confines of marriage. Any other use of sex is an abuse of sex.

A developing sex drive is often hard to understand—especially for teenagers whose glands and hormones are going crazy. Most teenage boys are convinced that they are sex maniacs because they think about sex a great deal. Marketing experts are aware that "sex sells." That's why the media constantly bombards us with advertising filled with sexual messages.

We have to control and properly direct our sexual urges because Satan always takes our God-given desires and tries to make us fulfill them in sinful ways. Sigmund Freud wasn't far from the truth when he said that just about every hang-up and problem we experience could be traced back to our powerful sex drives. What Freud didn't understand is that God has already given us His way to have an outlet and fulfillment for our sexual urges: One woman and one man committed to each other in a monogamous, marital relationship for life.

Our permissive society is another reason adultery is such a problem in America today. There really is no age limit for adultery. A wife once wrote a letter to Abigail Van Buren in which she said, "Dear Abby, I know boys will be boys, but my boy is seventy-three years old, and he is still chasing women. Do you have any suggestions?" Abby wrote back, "Don't worry; my dog has been chasing cars for years, but if he ever caught one, he wouldn't know what to do with it."

Our sexually saturated society constantly tries to convince us that any kind of sex is normal. In 2003, the Supreme Court repealed anti-sodomy laws, and Massachusetts became the first state in our nation to legalize same-sex marriage. Our culture is systematically dismantling the traditional, biblical understanding of marriage. It says you can practice sex with whomever you please, as long as both parties are consenting adults. This sexually-liberated society says to Bible-believing Christians, "You are a bunch of puritanical freaks. Don't try to impose your Bible-thumping, religious fanatic morality on me." Until this latest generation, America had always accepted the validity of the Ten Commandments—including this seventh commandment. For the last 40 years, however, our citizens have ignored this moral standard, and it's easy to see the moral mess in which we now find ourselves. Instead of becoming sexually free, we have a nation of people who are slaves to pornography and sensuality.

Dr. Joyce Brothers is a celebrity psychologist. For years, she took the traditional view that adultery was harmful and destructive to a marriage. Recently an article by UPI said she has changed her stance. Dr. Brothers said, "I changed my mind on the subject of adultery after listening to women all over the country. They said I was wrong about infidelity being destructive of marriage. With hundreds of women objecting to my previous stance, it was necessary for me to rethink my theory." Joyce Brothers may have rethought her theory, but God hasn't changed His mind about it. Dr. Brothers continues, "I don't begin to suggest that all married women should have affairs, but for those who feel unappreciated and unloved, sometimes an affair is the answer." Stop right there for a moment. Do you see the trap? What woman HASN'T felt unloved and unappreciated at some time?

In 1992, the *Murphy Brown* television show made television history when the main character, Murphy (a single woman), decided to have a child outside marriage—as if that were a normal family practice in America. The media ridiculed then Vice-President Dan Quayle when he publicly disagreed. He was not opposing single-motherhood, as some argued. He was, however, criticizing the message that an intelligent woman's best option was to eclipse marriage and the role of a father in order to produce a family. He stood up and said, "Hey! That is wrong. This goes against our family values." He became the laughing stock of America because he was willing to stand up for what the Bible says about a family in a time when out-of-wedlock births had reached an all-time high.

Peer pressure persuades Americans that they are unusual if they are faithful in marriage. I heard a pastor tell a true story about a women's meeting on the West Coast where the speaker was addressing the problem of infidelity among women and candidly asked every woman who had been sexually faithful to her husband to raise her hand. Only one woman (out of around 100 who were present) raised her hand.

However, that's not the end of the story. One wife went home, told her husband about the survey and said, "Only one woman raised her hand, and it wasn't me." Her husband raised his eyebrows, and she quickly said, "Wait! I assure you I have been faithful to you, but I was afraid that if I raised my hand, all my friends would think that I was a prude." Isn't it sad to see that we have come to be place where many Americans are embarrassed because they *keep* the seventh commandment?

How Can Adultery Be Avoided?

If you are reading this and have never committed physical adultery—good for you. However, don't be too proud, because those who think they are beyond sin become the easiest targets. Stay on guard. Even if you are guilty of violating the seventh commandment (either physically or mentally), you can start clean today. First, it will help you to recognize the suffering that comes from violating this commandment. Proverbs 6:32–33 says, *"But a man who commits adultery lacks judgment; whoever does so destroys himself. Blows and disgrace are his lot, and his shame will never be wiped away."* Any act of adultery is like dropping a pebble in a calm pool of water. The initial splash creates ripples that expand across the entire pool.

When you commit adultery, you not only damage yourself, you hurt your spouse, your children, your friends, your church and your community. Adultery creates a concentric circle of suffering from the epicenter of disobedience.

Sometime ago I read an article advocating if more men would watch the movie, *Fatal Attraction,* there would be less adultery. In this movie, a crazy woman became so obsessed with a married man that she wouldn't let him break off their affair. She emotionally tortured and physically attacked him and his family. I would revise the statement about seeing that movie. I believe if more men would read the Word of God, there would be less adultery.

The Bible is not really a "G" rated book that attempts to censor sexual sin. There is no attempt to cover up the many examples of immorality. The Bible contains many stories about the moral failures of men and women. It also speaks clearly about the terrible consequences they suffered because of their disobedience.

Remember King David, the sweet shepherd who sang beautiful psalms to God? The Bible says that he was a man after God's own heart. In spite of this, he suffered a horrible moral lapse. The Bible doesn't try to cover up and make him appear as some perfect saint. Instead, it describes how he broke both the sixth and seventh commandment. He committed adultery with Bathsheba and then murdered her husband.

Did he get away with it? Absolutely not! For a while, he thought he did, but then God sent the prophet Nathan to incriminate him. When David repented of his sins, God forgave him. However, David still had to suffer the terrible consequences of his sin. What happened? The baby conceived from their sexual affair died, and David grieved immensely. However, soon three more of David's children would die violent deaths. God will forgive our sin, but He doesn't remove the consequences of our poor choices.

You may object at this point and say, "Wait a minute. My God is so loving, compassionate and forgiving. He would never do anything like that to me." You must be careful not to impose a false sense of sentimentality upon God. God is love, but love is often tough. God is holy and pure, and He will forgive all sins. However, consequences remain. God is God, and He can do whatever He wishes. Hebrews 12 reminds us that God loves whomever He chastens, just as any loving parent would do (12:5–11). *"My son, do not make light of the Lord's discipline, and do not lose heart when he rebukes you, because the Lord disciplines those he loves, and he punishes everyone he accepts as a son"* (12:5).

If you are involved in any kind of willful, continual disobedience, whether it is adultery, sexual sin or anything else, God will first warn you. He rebukes before He chastens. If you don't repent of your sin, according to Hebrews 12, God will "chastise" (punish) you. You WILL suffer the consequences, and those around you may suffer as well.

Take Precautions

Some people have been so confused that they try to rationalize their sinful behavior. They reason that since they have already committed adultery in their minds, they might as well go all the way. Wrong! The consequences of committing adultery by fantasy are a great deal less severe than the increased consequences of the act itself. You can confess mental adultery to God and nobody else knows about it— even the person who is the object of the lustful thoughts. God will forgive and cleanse your heart and change your mind. But, if the thought becomes a temptation, then a fantasy, then an act, then a habit, it soon becomes a lifestyle. At that point, you and many other people will suffer the horrific consequences. The best place to stop adultery is BEFORE the thought takes hold in your mind.

Perhaps the best way to avoid adultery (or any sexual sin) is to refuse to entertain evil thoughts. Sin starts in your mind. So, if you can control your thought life, you have taken the first step in gaining control over sexual sin. You have several "gates" or "doors" into your mind, so be careful what you allow to enter. The number one avenue for pornography to enter our homes today is through the internet. It's private, often unsolicited and it's addicting more men and women every year. Don't listen to the wrong kind of music. Treat sexual television shows and movies like the plague. Be careful that you don't read books that inspire wicked thoughts. Only allow good, clean things to enter your mind. If you don't commit adultery in your mind, you won't commit it with your body.

America's 10 billion per year porn industry is destroying families and threatening our society's survival. If you are involved in any kind of pornography, I have a simple solution for you. Get rid of it. Whether it is pornography on videos, in magazines or on the internet in the privacy of your own home, stop it. Exposing yourself to pornography is like throwing lighted matches into a barrel of gasoline, although many may argue that it is just "soft core" pornography. That is an oxymoron. A better word for it is "rotten" pornography because it is rotten to the core—and will soon make you rotten on the inside, too.

In 2 Corinthians 10:4–5, the Apostle Paul gives us some useful insight on how to defeat sexual temptation. *"The weapons we fight with are not the weapons of the world. On the contrary, they have divine power to demolish strongholds. We demolish arguments and every pretension that sets itself up against the knowledge of God, and we take captive every thought to make it obedient to Christ."* Your mind is the battleground of sexual temptation; you will win (or lose) the fight there. If you aren't vigilant, Satan will attempt to construct a "stronghold" (think of a fort) of sexual temptation in your mind. Through the mighty power of God, you can demolish that stronghold of sexual thoughts. The key is to recognize and capture those tempting thoughts and then turn them into servants for Christ. It could be as simple as forcing yourself to visualize Jesus hanging on the cross for you; that powerful scene will usually make those evil thoughts disappear.

Another step you can take to avoid adultery is to recognize dangerous settings and run from them before the temptation becomes intense. You should be careful that you don't allow yourself to be placed in any kind of compromising situation. In 2 Timothy 2:22 Paul says, *"Flee from youthful lust or desires."* During moments of clear thinking and control, you must set some standards for yourself. You must decide what you WON'T and what you WON"T watch. Stick by these standards and don't compromise. Don't wait until you smell smoke from the fires of sexual temptation and passion to make those kinds of decisions.

When I was a youth minister, I told teenagers that the time to decide to be sexually pure is NOT when you are in the back seat of a car fogging up the windows. The time to decide to be sexually pure is when you are thinking calmly, rationally and reasonably. When I counseled teenagers, I told the girls, "Put a Bible between you and your date, so you can tell him he will have to go through Matthew, Mark, Luke and John before he can get to you."

Joseph is a great example of how to resist sexual temptation (Genesis 39:1–23). When Potiphar's wife propositioned him repeatedly, he just ran away. Once she even grabbed him, but he ran, leaving her holding his coat. Even though he suffered for his resistance by going to prison, God approved him. Sometimes, the best thing to do is to simply get up and run away from a potential trouble spot.

Studies have shown that most adulterous relationships formulate in the workplace. If you work with the opposite sex, you need to set some clear standards. For a start, don't be alone with a person of the opposite sex. For example, don't ride alone with him or her in a car or have a meal with only that person. This may sound old fashioned, but it is for your own protection.

What's the Positive Side of This Command?
What is God's positive alternative for adultery? Is God so mean that He wants to keep you from enjoying sexual pleasure in life? No, not

at all! In fact, He is trying to help you enjoy it to the fullest. Paul says in Hebrews 13:4, *"Marriage should be honored by all, and the marriage bed kept pure, for God will judge the adulterer and all the sexually immoral."* Physical intimacy in marriage is the sole reason God created sex. Here are two standards that will ensure that you will experience God's best for your life.

Maintain Purity until Marriage

Whether you are a single adult, a teenager or a college student, sexual purity until marriage is God's design for your life. "True Love Waits" is more than just a nice slogan from Focus on the Family's campaign; it is a great goal in life. When you are a teenager, you have all kinds of thoughts about sex. If you make the mistake of experimenting with sex before marriage, you will one day look back and regretfully say, "If only I had stayed pure." I've never met a husband or wife who said, "I'm glad I wasn't a virgin when I got married." However, I've heard dozens lament, "I wish I had stayed pure until I married my spouse. We would have avoided so many problems."

When I was a college student, I went to Panama City Beach with Campus Crusade for Christ during spring break. We were out on the beaches sharing the Gospel with all the students who were there to party. I saw this guy with a message on his shirt that said: STAMP OUT VIRGINITY. I was so angry about the message on his shirt that I wanted to rip it off his body. However, one of my friends took a different approach. He said, "Man, that's a really cool shirt. You ought to save it until you get married and have kids. Then if you have a daughter, let her wear it on her first date." This guy didn't have much to say in response.

Maintain Loyalty in Marriage

What is God's word for those who are married? You must maintain sexual loyalty to your spouse ... until death do us part! When commenting on marriage, Jesus said, *"What God has joined together, let man not separate"* (Mark 10:9).

I'm part of the "baby boomer" generation. Seventy-one million of us were born between 1946 and 1964. As most of us are now past middle age and approaching retirement, we hold the record of having more divorces than any other generation in history. We have believed a lie about romance and marriage. Some of the songs we grew up with had lyrics like, "Oh it's sad to belong to someone else when the right one comes along." Remember "Torn between two lovers, feeling like a fool. Loving both of them is breaking all the rules"? What a lie these songs put into our minds! They communicate that somewhere out there is a "Mr. Right" or "Miss Right." If we married the <u>wrong</u> one and later in our marriage, we find the <u>right</u> one, we must correct our mistake. We must get rid of this one and marry the right one. I know some people who have tried six and seven times to find the "right" one.

Here's the truth. When you married your spouse, he or she <u>became</u> the right one. Once you make a vow to restrict your romance to your mate, that settles it. Sure, you can always find someone else out there who lights your fire and turns you on and makes you feel as you did when you were a teenager—but in a good marriage, you STOP LOOKING.

A Good Love Triangle

We often consider a "love triangle" as some kind of an illicit relationship, but this idea is actually a requirement for a successful marriage. Try it. Imagine a marriage triangle where Jesus is placed at the apex, and you and your mate are at the two bottom corners. As each of you moves up the sides of the triangle, the closer you will be to Jesus and the closer you will be to each other. It's also true that the farther away from Jesus you are, the more distance you experience from your mate. When both of you are content in Jesus, you will experience true unity, and you will discover the kind of relationship God intended for you from the start.

You may feel terrible at this point because you realize that you have already failed in the area of sexual purity. You may be unmarried and have had sex. If you have, God will forgive you—but you must confess this behavior as sin and stop it immediately. That's what it means to repent of sin. If you are married and have committed adultery, God will forgive you. But you must break off that relationship and repent of that sin.

You may not yet be in an improper sexual relationship, but you are in the formative stages of it. You are already past the fantasy stage and are planning how you can approach that person. God is trying to tell you to save yourself and others who love you a world of heartache and pain. Stop it. You may need to change jobs to flee from this temptation. Do whatever it takes to break off the relationship. If you have been guilty, and sincerely repent, you can find cleansing. Jesus says the same thing He said to a woman who was caught in adultery, "Neither do I condemn you, go now and leave your life of sin" (John 8:10).

Even with the recent discouraging developments in our court system, the "sexual revolution" in America will ultimately continue to fail. It will only create more disease, depression and despair. America will never regain her greatness until we decide that we will follow God's perfect plan for sexual purity until marriage and sexual purity in marriage.

CHAPTER 8

"Nobody Will Ever Know"

"You shall not steal."
Exodus 20:15

Several years ago when Pope John Paul visited the U.S., he toured some of the seedy areas of one of our largest cities. When asked what he thought about what he'd seen, his remark was classic, "I'm afraid we are going to need a few more commandments." We may feel that way sometimes, but the ten God has given us are adequate to bring order, direction and purpose in our lives. Even the shortest of the commands contains volumes of insight.

Most Americans have been robbed at some time in their lives—a house broken into, a car stolen or private property stolen. In addition, it's also true that most Americans have stolen at one time in their lives. It might have been a piece of gum as a child, a towel or ashtray from a hotel or a grape from the produce section of the grocery store. Maybe you disagree with the title of this chapter. You have stolen something in the past, and you have "gotten away with it." Wrong. Someone always knows. If not in this life or this place, God knows.

Whether you are the victim of stealing or the guilty party, you can learn some truths from the Word of God about how to deal with theft.

The Heart of the Problem

You need to understand that people are not thieves because they steal; people steal because they are thieves. Think about that statement. In every human heart, there is the potential for criminal depravity. We all possess a tendency to sin. As we saw in chapter 6, Jesus said that all kinds of sin (including theft) come from within the human heart. Someone has well stated, "The heart of the human problem is the problem of the human heart."

Do you recall the Rodney King case from the early 90s? The Los Angeles police were seen beating motorist Rodney King on amateur video. When taken to trial, the police officers were found innocent. When the Rodney King verdict was announced, people literally went wild and started looting stores and burning property—all on live television. Joyous people carried televisions, refrigerators and stereos through broken store windows.

Jesus said that each of us has within our heart the potential for that kind of behavior. That kind of conduct is merely symptomatic of the human depravity that we all share. The Bible says in Jeremiah 17:9, *"The heart is deceitful above all things and beyond cure. Who can understand it?"* God is the only one who understands the sinful human heart.

Greed Motivates Theft

One reason people steal is simply that they are greedy and selfish. They just want more and more of something—money, property or anything else that can be stolen. The sinful human nature says in effect, "I'm going to take what I do not have. It's not right for someone else to have so much, so I will correct this imbalance." The Bible speaks to that very clearly in Ephesians 4:28, *"He who has been stealing must steal no longer, but must work, doing something useful with his own hands, that he may have something to share with those in need."* The antidote for theft is hard work.

There are two legitimate ways that you can obtain goods or money. You can work for it or you may receive it as a gift. Any other way of obtaining possessions is outside the will of God. When you think about robbery, you may picture a hold-up at a bank or store. But stealing minor items from work or a friend's house also violates this commandment.

It is not the amount being stolen that makes one a thief—but the act itself. Stealing violates a fundamental human right that God has given us—the right to have private property. If I own something and you are stronger, you must respect my rights and not steal it from me. Basic human dignity is tied up in the right to private property.

Charles Darwin, the father of the theory of evolution, promoted the concept of "the survival of the fittest" where only the strong survive. In a culture where anarchy rules, the strongest are the ones who get all the goods. American philanthropists are often frustrated when food is sent to hungry people in Third World countries. The strong-armed dictators or their cronies often claim the goods and try to sell them. However, this "survival of the fittest" practice happens in America, too. It usually starts in the playground in kindergarten when the stronger kids push down the weaker kids to get what they want. Then it carries over into the halls of high school where the bullies push their weight around. This greedy principle graduates into the offices of many skyscrapers and rears its ugly head in what is often called "hostile takeovers." Part of being civilized and living together is the understanding that "I respect your property and you respect my property." That is why God set forth this command.

When I was young, my mother said something that I have struggled with for years. She said, "I don't believe we ought to steal, but if my children were starving, I would go into a grocery store and steal food." I thought it sounded noble at the time, but I started thinking about it. Does God set forth situational ethics? Is He saying it is wrong to steal most of the time, but there are *some times* we can steal? Has God set down a standard that He allows to be broken at times? No. It is NEVER right to do wrong, even if we can justify it in our own minds.

David said in Psalm 37:25, *"I was young and now I am old, yet I have never seen the righteous forsaken or their children begging bread."* If we trust God and follow Him, He will make sure we never have to beg for bread or steal for bread to eat. When we are tempted to steal to any degree in order to meet our basic needs, we must trust God to provide instead of taking the matter into our own hands.

The evidence of greedy theft is all around us. That's why we have keys and burglar alarms. Every key is a testimony of the sinful, depraved human heart. If no one stole, there would be no need for keys.

Stealing for the Thrill

Some steal, not because they are greedy, but because stealing gives them a thrill. It's a challenge to get away with it. They thrive on the excitement and adrenalin it produces.

The Bible says in Proverbs 9:17, *"Stolen water is sweet; food eaten in secret is delicious!"* That's not a biblical principle to follow; instead, it is an observation of the fallen nature of humanity. There's just something exciting about enjoying that which has been obtained without lawfully paying for it.

The American Retail Association recently stated that in every retail store, 1 out of 52 customers is shoplifting. In other words, if you go into a store and there are more than 50 people there, you can be assured that one out of that 50 is probably shoplifting. Every year one billion dollars worth of goods is stolen from retail merchants. The rest of us pay 25% higher prices because of theft. We end up paying for the merchandise that the shoplifters take. Many of these thieves are not stealing because they need or want the goods; they just like the thrill of stealing.

Perhaps you are aware of the case of the Hollywood celebrity who was arrested in the Beverly Hills' shopping district—one of many recent celebrity shoplifting incidents. She robbed a store of a $89 sweater, although she had $1400 cash in her purse. She told the police, "Life is boring. I did it just for the thrill of it."

There are certain gangs and clubs whose initiation rites include going into a store and ripping off a certain amount of goods. Another symptom of America's moral disintegration is that many have reached the point where they are stealing without even thinking about it. They justify stealing a towel from the hotel because they feel they are being overcharged to stay there.

I once saw a dramatic skit that started out with a man shaving in his bathroom at home. He had a towel around his neck and he was facing the audience as if he was looking into his bathroom mirror. His teenage daughter comes skipping in and says, "Dad! Dad! It is my lucky day!"

The father says, "Why is it so lucky?"

She replies, "I was just down at the local store and I gave the clerk a $10 bill for some groceries and she thought I gave her a $20 bill so she gave me too much change. It's my lucky day."

Her father stops shaving and shouts, "How dare you do that! Am I raising a thief? You march right back down there and give back that money."

As she solemnly walks out, he mumbles, "I don't know what's happening to this younger generation." Then as he turns around the audience sees that the words "Holiday Inn" are printed on the towel he had wrapped around his neck.

Cheating Is Lying and Stealing

There is a funny story about a butcher who used a wooden meat barrel filled with ice to keep the meat fresh. It was near the end of the day and a woman came in wanting a chicken for supper. He reached into the barrel and found only one chicken. He pulled it out and said, "How is this?"

She replied, "No, that's not big enough."

The dishonest butcher replaced that chicken and unsuccessfully felt around in the ice for another chicken. Thinking he could fool the customer, he brought out the same chicken and said, "Here's a bigger one, how's this?"

The customer said, "Fine. I'll take both of them."

What isn't so funny is the increase of all kinds of fraud in America. Robbery by fraud, often called "white collar" crime, is the most costly type of theft in America—costing our nation about 300 billion dollars annually. Proverbs 11:1 says, *"The Lord abhors dishonest scales, but accurate weights are his delight."* Even back in Bible times, there were merchants who were cheating their customers by using scales that were dishonest. Today, white collar crime is even more sophisticated and includes computer/internet fraud, credit card fraud, telemarketing fraud, money laundering, tax evasion, mail fraud and insider trading. Whether it is cheating in school, cheating in business, being deceptive about an expense report or trying to get more out of your customers than they ought to pay, it is fraud, and it is a violation of the eighth commandment.

For example, consider the fraudulent schemes of some multi-millionaire CEOs who used to head several large corporations. At the same time that they were contemplating corporate bankruptcy, the heads of certain companies were sinking millions into real estate, extravagant parties and bonuses to keep themselves financially afloat.

Another example is retail merchants who are sometimes guilty of a promotional scheme called "bait and switch." They will advertise an inexpensive product of which they only have one or two items to get the customer into the store so that they can sell them a more expensive item. That is false advertising—a form of stealing.

But retailers and large corporations are not the only guilty ones. You as an individual may also violate this commandment by falsifying insurance claims, for example. If you get more than you really deserve, you might justify it by saying that insurance companies have plenty of money and won't miss another hundred dollars or so. That constitutes fraud. It is as if you went into a store with a gun and said, "Give me a hundred dollars." It's robbery with a pencil instead of with a gun. Even the "little" things like using the company phone lines to make personal long-distance calls or chatting with friends or surfing the web while "on the clock" constitute stealing.

If you try to cheat the IRS on your income tax, you are violating this commandment. If you put down information that is not true or leave out important data, you are stealing from the government. You may think that nobody ever knows about it. You may fool the IRS, but God knows about it. You can't deceive Him.

Students who cheat on exams at school are stealing because they are getting something (a better grade) that they really don't deserve. Again, it is the same thing as holding a gun to the teacher's head and demanding that you be given a good grade. God is aware of every single episode of cheating in school, from copying an answer on a test to downloading whole term papers for sale on the internet.

When I was a student in seminary, I had a certain professor who did an unusual thing. He said, "Here is your mid-term test. I want you to take it home and in the privacy of your home, complete it, but I don't want you to use your book. This is NOT an open book test."

Someone asked, "Wait a minute. Since we are going to be at home when we take the test, who is to stop us from using our textbook? Who will know whether or not we will open our book to get the answers?"

The wise professor replied, "God will know. Moreover, you will know. That's enough. It's important for you to learn early in your ministry whether or not you are going to be a cheater."

You may be thinking that you are innocent of breaking this eighth commandment. Take a moment and examine your life. If you have been cheating in any of these areas, you have been receiving something that is not rightfully yours. This kind of deceptive theft must be confessed to God ,and restitution should be made.

Are You Robbing God?

One of the most serious forms of robbery is found in Malachi 3:8–10. God says, *"Will a man rob God? Yet you rob me. But you ask, 'How do we rob you?' In tithes and offerings. You are under a curse—the whole nation of you—because you are robbing me. Bring the whole tithe into the storehouse, that there may be food in my house. Test me in this, says the Lord Almighty, and see if I will not throw open the floodgates of heaven and pour out so much blessing that you will not have room enough for it."*

Tithing is returning 10% of your income to God. It is not the highest attainment in the Christian life. I would not even put it as one of the top-ten things a Christian could or should do. Tithing is an elementary achievement in the course of Christian growth. It's like learning multiplication tables or writing in cursive. You learn those skills so that you can perform other educational tasks. Tithing is the same way. Tithing is a basic area of obedience that allows you to experience bigger and better things with the Lord. It is a spiritual prerequisite for other areas of blessing. Some people think, "Well, if I can just start tithing, I will have really arrived in my Christian life." Tithing is NOT a finish line; it's like a starting point. God says it is an absolute basic of the Christian life.

When there seems to be "something wrong" in your Christian life, you should examine the following personal checklist:

- Is there unconfessed sin in my life?
- Am I praying daily?
- Am I studying the Bible on a regular basis?
- Am I sharing my faith with those who don't know Christ?
- Am I faithful in worshiping God with other believers?
- Am I robbing God? Am I withholding my first ten percent of my income to the Lord on a regular basis?

God wants to bless you, but He can't do that if there are areas of willful disobedience in your life. Once you begin to be faithful in these basic areas, you will find that God will bestow tremendous blessings on you. In the area of tithing, God says, *"Test me and see if I won't open the windows of heaven and pour out a blessing so great you cannot contain it."* While the Scripture makes it clear that God often tests us, this is the ONLY time in the entire Bible where God invites us to put Him to the test. You'll never know the joy of that promise until you stop robbing God and start tithing.

Several years ago, I was preaching a revival in a small church in Alabama. On Tuesday morning of the revival, the pastor and I were coming into the church when we heard the church secretary weeping. We rushed into the office and saw that someone had forced opened the office door, broken the lock on the filing cabinet and stolen Sunday and Monday's offerings. Can you believe that someone would burglarize a church?

Once I was returning late at night from a preaching engagement and I saw one of our church buses pass me. I knew no one was supposed to be out with the bus at that time of night, so I called the police to report a stolen bus. Sure enough, somebody had stolen the bus and driven it to Florida. (It's hard to hide a bus that has the church's name on the side!)

How do you feel about people who break into a church office and steal the offering? How do you feel about somebody who would steal a vehicle from the church? You may be thinking those people have sunk pretty low into the swamp of moral depravity.

However, Malachi 3:8 says that if you aren't tithing, you are in the same category as those who steal from a church. In both cases, we rob God.

Please understand—God doesn't need your money. He has all the riches He needs (does He even need anything?). Nevertheless, you and I desperately need God's blessing on our lives. If you've been robbing God, confess it as sin and start tithing.

Is There Any Hope for a Thief?

Maybe you realize at this point that you have broken the eighth commandment. Is there any hope? Certainly. We have a wonderful precedent in the life of a thief named Zacchaeus. Zacchaeus was a tax collector who fraudulently demanded more money from the people than they were supposed to give. He had stolen from them, and when he met Jesus, there was a change in his life. Zacchaeus stood up and said to the Lord, "Look Lord, here and now I give half of my possessions to the poor and if I have cheated anybody out of anything, I will pay back four times the amount" (Luke 19:8).

If you've cheated, deceived or stolen, there are some good guidelines for you to follow:

1. Admit it. Come clean with God. Confess it to your "priest," Jesus (Hebrews 8:1).
2. Make restitution. Pay back what you have taken.
3. Change your behavior. It is not enough to admit it and make restitution; you need to change your behavior.

When I was in the eighth grade, I was a member of the Student Council in the little school I attended in South Alabama. Our Student Council Store sold school supplies to the students. Every day, it was my job to take a cardboard box full of these supplies to each classroom to sell to the younger grades. I'm very embarrassed about it, but I began to steal some of the money that I collected. From time to time, I would take a quarter or two and slip them into my pocket. After basketball or football practice, I would treat my friends to a drink. It was so easy for me to justify this behavior. I kept telling myself that I *should* be paid for doing this job. I never got caught and eventually forgot about the incident.

When I was 20 years old, I was in Youth Evangelism and was getting ready to preach in a small church. I was on my face praying and said, "Lord, if there is any area in my life that is not right or clean with you, would you please make it known to me right now." Guess what? He brought that incident to my memory. I said, "Lord, what do you want me to do?" Immediately, I was reminded of Zacchaeus. The next week, I wrote a letter to the principal of my old school. I confessed to him what I had done and enclosed a check for at least four times the amount I figured I had stolen. I asked him to put it into the treasury of the Student Council. God impressed upon me that He could not further His blessing on my life until I was willing to make restitution.

It's All about Lordship

When you steal something, you are saying, "These 'things' are more important to me than God." Jesus said, *"You cannot serve both God and Money."* (Matt. 6:24) You must choose—is Jesus your Lord, or are money and possessions your Lord? If you go through life grabbing for more and more "stuff," you will come to a sad and bitter end.

Several years ago I read about a tragic event in the *Oklahoma City Times* newspaper. A fire broke out in an apartment complex in Oklahoma City and most of the people had escaped without injury. The firefighters were trying to contain the fire, but it was raging out of control. Suddenly one of the residents cried out, "Oh, my God! My baby is still in there!"

She thought someone else had brought her baby out, but when she looked around, she realized that her child must still be inside the apartment. She tried to run back into the apartment to save her baby, but strong and compassionate arms constrained her. Although it was much hotter and much more dangerous than the firefighters liked to risk, one firefighter entered the burning complex.

He put on his oxygen mask and protective clothing, and his fellow firefighters sprayed him down with water before he walked into the smoke and flames. The heavy smoke made it nearly impossible to see, but he managed to find the bedroom of that apartment. In a few moments, he was seen staggering out with a blanket-covered bundle in his arms. The crowd cheered. The mother rushed up, took the bundle in her arms, opened the blanket and said, horrified, "This isn't my baby—this is my baby's doll."

Perhaps the only story more sad and tragic would be people who one day face God for all eternity and find that they risked everything for a bunch of toys. They grabbed onto a bunch of "things" in life and missed the real thing—knowing and serving God.

How can you relate to God's eighth moral standard in a positive way? Respect the property rights of others. Realize that if you don't WORK for something or receive it as a GIFT, you have obtained it by dishonest means. Exercising respect for others and good hard work are the best ways to obey this commandment.

CHAPTER 9

The Wicked Webs We Weave

"You shall not give false witness against your neighbor."
Exodus 20:16

The title of this chapter is taken from the familiar quote, "Oh what wicked webs we weave when first we practice to deceive." When you start telling lies, you must construct a flimsy network of additional lies to support the first one. Soon, you are so caught up in your own lies until you are trapped like a fly in a spider web. The ninth commandment can be violated by telling a lie— AND it can be violated when we speak against our neighbor.

God hates words that deceive. You may choke on the word "hate" because you know that God is love, and the idea of God hating anything or anybody is hard for you to swallow. However, read the following scripture for yourself.

Proverbs 6:16–19 says, *"There are six things the Lord hates, seven that are detestable to him: haughty eyes, a lying tongue, hands that shed innocent blood, a heart that devises wicked schemes, feet that are quick to rush into evil, a false witness who pours out lies and a man who stirs up dissension among brothers."* Of the seven things listed that God hates, two of them have to do with the ninth commandment. God cannot stand lying. Why is that? The very character of God is that of truth. Any kind of deception or lie is an insult to His truthful character.

Imagine that a concert artist is asked to play a piano concert. He enters the concert hall dressed in a tuxedo, complete with tails. He walks to the piano, flips up the tail of his tux, sits down and begins to play a well-known concerto. However, he discovers in the first few bars that the piano is terribly out of tune. That artist would be so offended that he would stop playing. He would refuse to play on a piano that is out of tune. Even if the audience is willing to listen, he will refuse to offer sour music. Just as sour notes offend an expert musician, our God, who is truth incarnate, is offended when he hears His children speaking lies.

Every Lie Comes from Satan

Did you know there is a source or "father" of every lie? In John 8:44, Jesus tells us that Satan is the one who conceives every falsehood. He said, *"You belong to your father, the devil, and you want to carry out your father's desire. He was a murderer from the beginning, not holding to the truth, for there is no truth in him. When he lies, he speaks his native language, for he is a liar and the father of lies."*

When you lie, you are speaking the devil's language. Everything Satan has ever said has been a lie. Do you recall Satan's first recorded words in the Bible? He came to Eve in the Garden of Eden and asked, "Did God tell you that you couldn't eat of this particular fruit?"

"Yes, God said that if we touched it or ate it, we would die," Eve replied.

Then Satan said, *"You will not surely die. For God knows that when you eat of it your eyes will be opened and you will be like God, knowing good and evil"* (Genesis 3:4–5). What a lie! Instead of becoming wise, they experienced the evil that disobedience brings.

Today, the New Age movement promotes this ancient lie. The New Age movement tells us we can become our own God. There is nothing new about that; it's as old as Satan's first lie. It's an Old Age movement.

Satan will even try to lie to God. You can see this from a conversation that he had with God recorded in Job 1:11. God, observing all his servants, points out to Satan what a faithful servant

Job is. However, Satan says about Job, *"Stretch out your hand and strike everything he has and he will curse you to your face."* That was a lie. Job remained faithful despite his tragedies.

The devil even lied to the Lord Jesus. He took Jesus to a tall mountain and showed him the splendor of the kingdoms of the world. Then he made this offer, *"All this I will give you if you will bow down and worship me"* (Matthew 4:9). Do you think Satan could have really done that? Of course not! Everything he says is a lie. Of course, Jesus recognized that he was a liar and said, "Away from me, Satan." Satan is a liar. Every time you tell a lie, you are speaking the devil's language.

A Generation of American Liars

In contrast to God's disdain for lying, Americans possess a flippant attitude about lying. The attitude today is, "Hey, everybody lies, so what?" We expect to be lied to; that's why we have developed such a skeptical, cynical nature. Few people believe television commercials anymore because we suspect that the marketing experts are just lying again.

A few years ago, an automobile company, Isuzu, capitalized on our cultural skepticism. The leading representative in their commercials, a reptilian-looking character named Joe Isuzu, would look right into the camera, smile and proceed to lie outright. He would say, "You can get a brand new Isuzu car for only $9.95. It will go 300 miles per hour. If you buy an Isuzu now, you get a brand new home, free of charge." On the screen, you see the words, "He's lying" superimposed over his picture. Joe continues, "It gets 600 miles to the gallon." Of course we know he's lying, but their point was, "So is everyone else." At least they are admitting it. The commercials didn't last very long!

In 1991, American learned some shocking, but not so surprising, statistics in a survey of thousands of Americans that revealed: [viii]

- 91% of Americans lie routinely or nearly every day.
- 36% of the people confessed to dark, important lies.

- 86% of children said they lie to their parents.
- 75% of the people say they lie to their friends.
- One out of every three people in the workforce is working with a resume that reflects a lie.
- 33% of workers have misrepresented either their education or experience.

We are a generation of habitual liars, so what else is new?

The Bible says in Psalm 58:3, *"The wicked are estranged from the womb, going astray as soon as they are born, speaking lies."* Parents don't have to teach their children to lie; they just come by it naturally. Rather, children must be taught to tell the truth. At one time (or perhaps many times), ALL of us have told a lie, practiced deception or used exaggerations or embellishment. It takes only one lie to make a liar. Every lie offends God because it is a violation of His character of truth.

What's the Big Deal Anyway?

What is the fate of liars? Whether it is a little white lie, a medium gray lie or a big black lie, God hates it. To see how seriously God considers lying, look in Rev. 21:8. Notice the kind of sinners with which liars are grouped. *"But the cowardly, the unbelieving, the vile, the murderers, the sexually immoral, those who practice magic arts, the idolaters, and <u>all liars</u>—their place will be in the fiery lake of burning sulfur. This is the second death."*

God is so offended by lying that He ranks it with murder, sexual abuse, idolatry and drug abuse. The Bible says every liar is going to end up in hell. We are all liars, and what we deserve is eternal separation from God in a place called hell. That's what we **deserve**, but here is the **good news**—God loves you so much that He sent Jesus to die for your sins. That's the ONLY way a liar can go to heaven. If you come to God in faith and repentance, He will forgive your sin, and will give you a home in heaven forever and ever. However, if you go through life making excuses, trying to justify your lying, you are headed for a bleak destiny.

In the story of Pinocchio, his nose grew longer every time he told a lie. That effect, though embarrassing, was actually a gift in disguise. Pinocchio (and everyone else) knew immediately when a lie had been told. Have you ever wished you had an internal bell or buzzer that would go off every time you lied or used an exaggeration? You do have a resource like that—He is called the indwelling Holy Spirit of God. Jesus called Him "the Spirit of Truth." When you speak or live a lie, the Holy Spirit in you will warn you. If you are a Christian, you have to deny or suppress the Spirit of Truth every time you tell a lie.

In Acts 5, we read about Ananias and Sapphira. This couple was a part of the early Christians who lived in Jerusalem. The church was in the process of giving money to meet the needs of the members. During this early church stewardship campaign, everyone was bringing money to the church. Ananias and Sapphira sold a piece of property. When Ananias came and laid the money before the feet of the Apostle Peter, he said, "Here's the money from all that property I sold. This is the full amount." He was only telling a part of the truth—and that's lying.

He and his wife had actually kept some of the amount for themselves. It would have been perfectly acceptable if he had said, "Peter, this is half the money that I received from this property and I'm giving it to the church." Peter said, *"Ananias, how is it that Satan has so filled your heart that you have lied to the Holy Spirit? .... you have not lied to men, but to God."* (Acts 5:3–4) At that moment, Ananias fell down dead. Sometime later, Ananias' wife, Sapphira, came in (not knowing her husband's fate), told the same lie and died. That shows how seriously God deals with those who lie to Him.

We are all sinners; we are all liars. However, if we love God, we will love the things God loves and will hate the things God hates. Don't you hate to be lied to? Multiply that feeling ten billion times, and that is how God reacts.

Destructive Words Can Destroy People

There are two parts to this commandment. Not only is there a prohibition against deception, but the idea of speaking a word against our neighbor is included. We've already addressed the old adage about how "sticks and stones may break your bones, but words can never hurt you." If you've ever been hurt by someone's words, you may relate more to this revised version, "Sticks and stones cause wounds that heal, but hateful words are words that kill." Hateful words can destroy homes, marriages, families and careers.

One way you can violate the ninth commandment is by slander, which is like a verbal slap. The person doesn't even have to be present. You may be talking about him or to him. When we say something about somebody that is unkind, hateful, harmful—whether it is true or not—that is slander.

Proverbs 11:9 says, *"With his mouth the godless destroys his neighbor, but through knowledge the righteous escape."* The tendency on the part of Christians is to talk about people, especially when they are not there. What passes for "prayer requests" is often gossip covered in a cloak of spirituality. A.B. Simpson wrote, "I would rather play with forked lightning or take in my hand live wires with their fiery current than to speak a reckless word against any servant of Christ or to idly repeat the slanderous darts which thousands of Christians are hurling on others." The quality by which every Christian is truly judged is by love.

Gossip is receiving and/or passing on hateful, harmful information about another person. My mother always taught me, "If you cannot say something good about somebody, don't say anything at all." I agree with that. A gossip's motto is, "If you can't say something good about somebody, be sure to tell me first."

Sometimes gossipers complain, "I can't help it; I don't want to gossip, but people just tell me these things." Divulging gossip is not an honor. It says very little about you that they choose your ears as a garbage receptacle for their filth. Just as stealing is wrong and receiving stolen property is wrong, telling gossip is wrong, and receiving gossip is wrong. You don't want people dumping garbage in your yard, but that's what they are doing when they gossip to you—dumping garbage in your mind.

Someone has said that you need to treat gossip like a red wasp; either ignore it or kill it immediately. Try to do anything else, and you will get hurt.

I know of a physician in a small town whose practice was almost destroyed because one of the nurses in his office started telling some of his patients that he had an incurable disease. One at a time, they quietly requested their records and changed physicians. The truth was that he had gone in for a routine physical and had X-rays and told the nurse he had to go back for some follow-up X-rays. She assumed that he had a problem.

The truth was the X-ray machine had malfunctioned, and he had to have the X-rays redone. He was perfectly healthy, but a rumor almost destroyed his practice. The nurse didn't mean to hurt him, but her words caused irreparable damage to his practice.

There once was a bank teller in a small town that was passed over for promotion. In addition, she was almost fired because a member of the bank's board of directors had seen her coming out of a bar in a bad part of town late one night. He assumed certain things about her character. The truth was that she was on her way home from a wedding shower when her car broke down, and she went into that bar to call for someone to come and give her a ride. That was all. However, her reputation suffered damage by the unfounded rumors.

Rumors grow and develop a life of their own. Mark Twain wrote, "A lie will go half way around the world while truth is still putting on its shoes." Sad but true.

There was a small weekly newspaper in a little town that had an interesting misprint. The front-page news was usually about who had caught the biggest fish or killed the biggest rattlesnake that weekend or some other tidbit of community news. A certain woman, known as the biggest gossip in town, went to the hospital to have some surgery. The newspaper reported, *"Mrs. Smith is in Atlanta having a rumor removed from her throat."* That misprint makes a lot of sense. If you ever have a rumor in your throat, it ought to be removed.

Proverbs 26:20 says this about gossip, *"Without wood a fire goes out; without gossip a quarrel dies down."* Gossip, rumors and innuendo all comprise the kind of speaking that violates the ninth commandment.

Steven Olford tells the story about a woman who was spreading some ugly gossip about a pastor who had been in the community for a long time. These rumors were false, but they did terrible damage to the pastor's reputation. He spent the last years of his life trying to fight this rumor. Before he died, it was clearly proven that everything this evil gossip had been saying was a lie.

The woman went to the old pastor to apologize. She said, "I'm sorry for the lie that I told about you. I didn't know it wasn't true. Will you please forgive me?"

The hurting pastor replied, "Dear lady, I've already forgiven you, but there is one thing I want you to do for me."

The humbled woman said, "Anything. Just tell me what I can do."

He said, "I want you to take a feather pillow and go to the hill outside town, rip open the pillow and shake out all the feathers and let the wind take them. After about an hour, I want you to go and pick up all the feathers and put them back in the pillow and bring the pillow to me."

Sadly, she said, "I can't do that. The wind will have scattered those feathers so far that I couldn't possibly retrieve all of them."

He paused and said, "How true. And neither can you retrieve the words you've spoken. Although you've asked me to forgive you, your words can never be retracted."

A.B. Simpson once said, "You had better bite your tongue before you say anything unkind, hateful, harmful against another brother or sister in Christ."

Speak Truthful Words That Build up

God hates words that deceive and destroy, but we honor God by words that delight. That is the positive side of this commandment. He wants us to use words that build up, edify and delight other people. Don't use your mouth to lie; don't use your mouth for slander or gossip. Use your mouth to praise God and to build up other people.

Ephesians 4:15 says, *"Instead, speaking truth in love, we will in all things grow up into him who is the Head, that is, Christ."* That is your goal as a Christian—to not just speak the truth, but also speak it in love. Some use truth as a hammer and try to pound people over the head with it. Afterwards, they say, "Well, the truth hurts, doesn't it?" (Meaning: it hurt you and I'm glad it hurt you.) That may be speaking the truth, but there is no love there. Others think love means that you never speak the truth. Truth without love is nothing but cold justice, but love without truth is nothing by syrupy senti-mentality. As a Christian, you must always be speaking the truth, but make certain that you are speaking it in love.

Here are the characteristics of love according to the Bible:

"Love is patient, love is kind. It is not jealous, it is not boastful, it is not arrogant. It is not rude, it does not keep a list of wrongs, it does not rejoice at wrong, but it rejoices in the light. Love bears all things, believes all things, hopes all things, endures all things. Love never ends" (1 Corinthians 13:4–8). If you cannot speak the truth with all those characteristics, do not speak at all.

Before you speak, pause to *think* first. Have you ever heard the expression, "Putting your mouth in motion before your mind is in gear?" Someone else has said, "Anybody who thinks by the inch, but speaks by the yard, ought to be kicked by the foot." Another warning goes, "Make sure your mouth doesn't start writing checks that your mind can't cash." All of this is good advice.

What should you think of before you speak? Here's a simple way to remember what to T.H.I.N.K.:

T - Is it true? Before you say it, is it true? That's first and foremost, but that's not all. Just because it is true doesn't mean you HAVE to say it. Look for the other factors below.

H - Is it helpful? Is what you are going to say helpful to that person or someone else? Or is it going to hurt or harm him or her?

I - Is it inspiring? Is it going to bring a person closer to God?

N - Is it necessary? There are a lot of things you can say that are not necessary to say.

K - Is it kind?

You can apply that "think" test to everything you say in every relationship. Proverbs 16:24 speaks about the power of positive words: *"Pleasant words are a honeycomb, sweet to the soul and heal-ing to the bones."* God is honored when you use your mouth to praise Him and to build up others. Try it—it really beats lying and gossip.

If you are a Christian and you are guilty of living a lie or speaking lies, you need to say, "God, I apologize. I didn't realize how every single like I tell terribly offends your character." You need to follow that with a firm commitment to be a truth speaker, doing it in love. If you are practicing slander, you need to repent of it and say, "God, I will stop destroying other people's character. I will speak only kind words to build people up. I will speak the truth in love."

I Can't Keep the Ten Commandments!

We've discussed nine of the ten requirements for America's survival, and by now, you have probably noticed that it seems humanly impossible to keep the Ten Commandments. One of the main purposes of God's Ten Commandments is to show you how much you need Him. The Ten Commandments only remind us how often we lie, have lustful thoughts, say angry words and the like.

When it comes to the "perfection test," we are all failures. God's moral test is a pass/fail test. You can't say, "I make about a seventy and you are a sixty." You can't try to slip by with a C minus. Everybody fails. The Bible says we are all sinners.

It's also true that we are all going to stand before God and give an account for our sinfulness. Those who have admitted their sinfulness, repented of their sin and put their faith in what Jesus did on the cross, have been forgiven. God doesn't look at them as liars or adulterers or thieves anymore. He looks at them through the filter of the righteousness of Jesus Christ and says, "I have a home for you in heaven. Your name is written in the Lamb's Book of Life. You are my child."

However, for those who have rejected God's free offer of forgiveness, it's a sad picture. The Bible says that they will spend eternity separated from the holy God in a place of torment called hell. I used to say there were two kinds of people, believers and unbelievers, but I was corrected. Now, I understand there really is no such thing as an unbeliever. There are only believers and those we may call "pre-believers." In the future, everyone is going to believe. They may die without Christ, but they will stand before God, and at that moment, they WILL believe. However, this won't be a saving faith—only a regretting faith because it will be too late.

Now is the time to admit that you can never be good enough to earn God's acceptance. You can't keep the Ten Commandments. You can only claim the grace and mercy of God. And that's no lie.

CHAPTER 10

Keeping up with the Joneses

"You shall not covet your neighbor's house. You shall not covet your neighbor's wife or his manservant or maidservant, his ox or donkey, or anything that belongs to your neighbor."

Exodus 20:17

I'm convinced that God designs the order and arrangement of the Ten Commandments. The first four deal with our relationship with God, and the last six deals with our human relationships. I think God has intentionally bracketed the Ten Commandments with twin human weaknesses—materialism and idolatry. First, God says, "Don't have any other gods before me. I must be number one in your life." God knew from the beginning that our human nature is prone to substitute material possessions for a living God. Then He concludes by specifically warning against the greed that drives our desire to have other "gods."

In America, we are all trying to "keep up with the Joneses." That means that when we see our neighbor with more "stuff" than we have—it makes us want (covet) to have at least as much as they have. If they get a new car, we feel we need a new car, too. If we see a new plasma television being delivered to their house, we start scheming how we can get one. Much of our society in America is built upon this game of one-upmanship when it comes to material possessions. That's why God reserves the prohibition against greed for the last commandment—because we tend to remember some-one's last words. His final word is "don't covet."

The word "covet" is the Hebrew word *chamad,* which means to "have an intense desire" for something. Actually, there's nothing wrong with coveting—if you covet the proper thing. I might say to you, "I covet your prayers." There's certainly nothing wrong with that. It is the **object** of our covetousness that makes certain desires a sin.

The Seeds of Greed

As you are reading about coveting, you may easily substitute the word "greed." Have you ever wondered, "What is it about me that causes me to want more material items?" In the New Testament, it is very clear—we have **selfish** hearts. We are born with this selfish heart—you can even see that tendency in little children. If you put toddlers together with toys, they will grab a toy and say, "Mine!" If they see another toddler with a different toy, they will often try to take it away. The seeds of greed are there from the start.

This greedy tendency is addressed in 1 Timothy 6:10, *"For the love of money is a root of all kinds of evil. Some people, eager for money, have wandered from the faith and pierced themselves with many griefs."* Of course, there's nothing wrong with money itself. Money is morally neutral; it is just a measurement of value. However, when you love and crave more and more money, that desire can become your god, and it can lead to all kinds of evil.

> Money can buy a bed, but it cannot buy sleep.
> Money can buy books, but it cannot buy knowledge.
> Money can buy food, but it cannot buy an appetite.
> Money can buy cosmetics, but it cannot buy beauty.
> Money can buy a house, but it cannot buy a home.
> Money can buy medicine, but it cannot buy health.
> Money can buy amusement, but it cannot buy joy.
> Money can buy a crucifix, but it cannot buy a Savior.
> Money can buy a pew in a church, but it cannot buy
> a place in heaven.

Money falls short when it comes to the real needs of life. If you devote your life to accumulating more and more money and loving the things that money can buy, you've missed the main reason for living.

Another reason for this greed is that our hearts are so **shallow**. If your god is gold and your creed is greed, you really don't have room for God. Be careful because your shallow heart can soon become full with material desires. Jesus warned us when He said, *"Watch out. Be on your guard against all kinds of greed. A man's life does not consist of the abundance of his possessions"* (Luke 12:15). Your life should be so much fuller than simply spending 80 years working to acquire a lot of possessions.

I once saw this message on a church sign, *"The best things in life ... aren't things."* The context in which Jesus spoke the words in Luke 12:15 gives it even greater impact. An angry man had confronted Jesus to demand that Jesus tell his brother to share the family inheritance with him. Not much has changed in 2000 years because families are fractured and divided today over who gets the leftovers when somebody has died. Americans still struggle with the need for greed.

I heard a visiting preacher from South Africa talk about visiting the Dallas area. He was invited into the home of a wealthy Texan in a very affluent neighborhood. When the preacher found the home he was supposed to visit, he drove into the circle driveway of this massive home and saw four expensive automobiles and a large boat in the garage. He also noticed a pool and pool house in the back area.

After the hostess greeted him at the door, she led him to the sitting room where they could talk. There, he noticed a book on the table ironically entitled, *How to Find Happiness*. It was obvious that his hostess had been reading this book when he arrived.

He thought, "If money, cars, mansions, money or stock portfolios could produce happiness, this lady would certainly qualify!" Yet she was still searching for happiness.

Greed Leads to Trouble

Covetousness (greed) is actually a curse that can cripple the one who constantly wants more. Greed makes a person a victim of a vicious cycle of dissatisfaction. If your mission and goal in life is to get more things and to accumulate possessions, you will never be satisfied. If you get a new car, before long it gets a little dull or scratched, and you start noticing all the newer and shinier models on the street. You assumed that your new automobile would satisfy for a while, but it didn't. You buy a new home and think it is so wonderful, but if you aren't careful, you will start noticing that there is always another house that is bigger and better than yours. If "having the best" becomes the primary source of satisfaction in your life, you are cursed because you never will be satisfied.

Have you ever heard how they capture monkeys in the rain forests of South America? Someone cuts the top off a coconut and hollows out the meat and juice. Then they string a strong cord through a hole in the coconut and tie it to a tree. Inside the hollowed out coconut they place a morsel of food. The size of the hole in the top of the coconut is small enough for the monkey to get his hand in it, but when he grabs the food, his fist will not come out. Invariably, the monkey refuses to let go of the food so he is caught. All the monkey has to do is let go of the food, and he would be free. There is a lesson there for each of us. Many people are grasping tightly to their money and possessions; and this greed becomes a trap.

We read in 1 Timothy 6:9, *"People who want to get rich fall into temptation and a trap and into many foolish and harmful desires that plunge men into ruin and destruction."* The Bible says that if you want to head for ruin and destruction in this life, just let greed direct your life. All around you, our society is trying to entice you to buy more and to buy better. Some of the sharpest minds in America are on Madison Avenue in New York City, where most of the television commercials and print ads originate. Brilliant young adults are paid six-figure salaries to entice you to buy certain kinds of jeans, shirts, shoes, etc. They are directing all their creative talent to convince you that you can't be satisfied with just any old pair of jeans—you must have the right jeans. You can't buy just any pair of shoes—you simply have to have the brand that everyone else is wearing. From the time you start watching television until you die, you are being bombarded with pressure-slogans like "Buy now!" "This offer ends soon." "Take advantage of this once-in-a-lifetime deal."

I once saw an auto ad in the newspaper that epitomized the human desire for greed. The sticker price was $12,000, but this ad made a big deal about how you could go in that day, drive that car out with no down payment, and pay only $259 a month. I imagine there were some people who looked at that shiny red car and succumbed to the ad's message. However, when I read the "small print," it revealed that the buyer would be paying for that car for eighty-four months. That's seven years. Including interest, they would actually be paying over $20,000 for this basic, bottom-of-the-line car. Advertisers are required by law to add that disclaimer, but there is no requirement about the size of the print.

Of course, everybody needs transportation, but our whole Madison Avenue culture says to buy a better one, buy a new one and buy it now. This urge to buy the newer and better becomes a vicious circle of dissatisfaction. You start out with a Chevrolet, and you are not satisfied, so you get a Buick, and you are not satisfied, so you get an Oldsmobile, and you're not satisfied, so you get a Cadillac, and you are not satisfied, so you get a Lexus, and you are not satisfied, so finally you get a Mercedes—even if you have to mortgage your house. You are fine for a while until a Rolls Royce or a Jaguar passes you. You will never be satisfied if you get into this cycle of greed.

The One Who Dies with the Most Toys Wins

Some time ago, *USA Today* had an article about a new board game produced by Milton Bradley. The name of the game is *Mall Madness*. In this game, you are let loose in a shopping mall with $500. The goal is to spend it as fast as you can. When you have spent all your money, and you have moved your marker into the space labeled "broke," you win. Based on that game's philosophy, many Americans are winners.

This addiction to buying is something that has intensified over the last quarter of a century. A survey of teenage girls recently revealed that 93 % of them said their number one favorite pastime is shopping. Until three decades ago, the typical American "gathering place" was a church or a town square. In the last 25 years, the gathering place for our culture has become the American mall. Madonna captured the mood of our culture when she admitted that she was a "material girl living in a material world."

Perhaps you've seen the tee shirt that says, "The one who dies with the most toys, wins." That's the attitude of many Americans. However, I recently saw a message that was direct rebuttal to that attitude. It said, "The one who dies with the most toys... still dies." Greed can make you lose sight of God, and you become blinded to your own greed. When you are blinded by greed, you become blinded to God. The interesting phenomenon about the tenth commandment is that very few people have ever admited being guilty of it.

Francis Xavier was a Catholic Priest after whom *Xavier University* is named. He heard confessions for 45 years. Father Xavier said he had heard confessions regarding nearly every sin in the Bible (and some NOT in the Bible). However, he said that in 45 years he had never heard one person confess the sin of covetousness. What is the reason for that? Covetousness can easily blind you, and it's impossible to see that you are like a bee that drowns in honey.

Is More and Bigger Better?

In Luke 12, Jesus told a story about a rich farmer who had a great increase in his crops. Because he was so successful, the farmer made plans to expand and then to retire in leisure. He said, *"This is what I'll do. I will tear down my barns and build bigger ones, and there I will store all my grain and my goods. And I will say to myself, 'You have plenty of good things laid up for many years. Take life easy; eat, drink and be merry'"* (Luke 12:18–19).

According to Jesus, God appeared to that farmer and said, *"You fool! This very night your life will be demanded from you. Then who will get what you have prepared for yourself?"* (Luke 12:20). This farmer had spent all his life accumulating material possessions and was wealthy; but in his spiritual life, he was empty—living in abject poverty. Then Jesus shared the warning to every one of us. He said, *"This is how it will be for anyone who stores up things for himself but is not rich toward God"* (Luke 12:21). You must make an important decision about your life. Is your goal to be rich toward God? If so, there can be no place for materialistic greed.

Don't Substitute Stuff for the Savior!

Another curse of greed is that a greedy person will often substitute "stuff" or material possessions for Jesus. Several years ago, someone suggested that for insurance purposes, I should video all our material property and catalog each item. That way, if a fire or storm damaged our house, replacing the property would be much simpler. I was shocked at how much "stuff" we have accumulated in over 25 years of marriage. As a result of that videotape, my wife and I immediately gave away much of our clothes and furniture to a benevolent ministry.

If you have traveled in any third world country, you realize that Americans live in relative luxury. Compared to every nation (except perhaps Switzerland or Germany), we are a wealthy nation. Even the poorest people in my city live better than most of the people in third world countries. In many of these countries, the daily concern is to find enough to eat or drink. Few Americans have to worry about that on a daily basis. Instead, we are more concerned with designer labels or the kind of cars we drive.

There is nothing wrong with stereos, cars, furniture and houses. These possessions are intrinsically neutral. However, if any possession becomes a substitute for Jesus, that material desire can be fatal. Anytime we substitute something nonessential for something that is essential for life, we make a dangerous exchange. For instance, there is nothing wrong with combing your hair, but if you suddenly substitute combing your hair for breathing, combing your hair will soon kill you. In the same way, possessions won't hurt you unless you substitute them for knowing Jesus. If you "possess your possessions" that's fine. However, if your "possessions possess you," then you are in danger of breaking this commandment.

The Antidote for the Poison of Greed

What is the good news when it comes to curing greed? First, you must establish your **contentment** in Christ. The word "contentment" means to be satisfied. Hebrews 13:5 says, *"Keep your lives free from the love of money and be content with what you have, because God has said, `Never will I leave you; never will I forsake you.'"* It doesn't say to be content with **who** you are, but be content with

what you have. Some people think that contentment means that they can just idle in "spiritual neutral gear." They think it means that they don't have to read the Bible or witness. No! You should be content with what you have, but you should never be content with who you are. Of course, you are IN CHRIST if you are a Christian, and you are content there (that's **positional** righteousness). However, the desire for **practical** righteousness means that you should possess a tremendous ambition to be all God wants you to be.

Ernest Hemingway was one of the most respected and gifted writers of this century. Before his death he wrote, "Life is just a dirty trick, a short journey from nothingness to nothingness. There is no remedy for anything in life. Man's destiny in the universe is like a colony of ants on a burning log." Not long after that, he committed suicide. Hemmingway seemed to have it all. He was famous, wealthy and respected, but he was miserable. He tried to find contentment in a bottle, drugs, success and wealth—but he never secured it.

In contrast to Hemingway, consider the old Nazarene preacher, Bud Robinson, who lived a couple of generations ago. Everyone affectionately called him Uncle Bud. He spoke with a lisp, but he was a mighty preacher. He once visited New York City to preach. While there, he toured all the famous sights—Times Square, Grand Central Station, the Empire State Building and Wall Street. That night, when he stood to preach, he said in his lisping voice, "Lord, I thank you that you let me thee all these things, but Lord, most of all, I thank you that I didn't thee a thingle thing I wanted." His contentment was not in great cities or wealth; his contentment was in Jesus Christ.

Are You Satisfied?

Can you say, "I am actually satisfied with what I have now"? Do you know why God says in the first commandment, "Thou shall have no other gods?" If we enthrone money, greed or possessions as our god, it will only lead to dissatisfaction. Because when life gets tough, these "gods" cannot help. When you make Jesus the only source of your satisfaction, you will never be disappointed.

Do you want to know how rich you are? Do you want to know how to calculate your spiritual net worth? Add up everything you own that money can't buy and death can't take away. That is how rich you are. The only aspect of your earthly life that gets sweeter and more precious as you move toward eternity is your relationship with Jesus Christ. Think about the possessions that are important to you now—houses, cars, land, savings accounts, and stock portfolios. In a thousand years from now, how much will they mean to you? On the other hand, in a thousand years, your relationship with Jesus Christ will be much more precious than it is now.

Replace Covetousness with Commitment

Another cure for greed is to deepen your commitment to Christ. You must let others know that Jesus is your source of contentment. As the apostle Paul said in Philippians 1:21, *"For to me to live is Christ and to die is gain."* How would you complete this statement? "For to me to live is _____." You fill in the blank. What word can you substitute for Christ and still consider it gain?

Here are some of the more popular options in America. Like others, are you saying: For me to live is **family**? Then to die would be LOSS because you will not have the same relationship even though they may be saved. For me to live is **money**? Then to die will be LOSS—because you can't take any of it with you. They use gold for pavement in heaven! For me to live is **education**? Then to die is LOSS because you can have more degrees than a thermometer, but if you don't know Jesus, it won't help you after you die. For me to live is **success in my business**? Then to die is LOSS—because your business success is worth nothing when you die. I have sat beside several dozen people as they were preparing to die, and I have never heard one of them say, "If only I had spent more time on my business." The ONLY word you can put in the blank (if you hope to **gain** when you die) is **Christ**. That's what Paul said, "For me to live is **Christ**—and to die is **gain**."

In Philippians 1:21, it's as if Paul is tossing a coin and saying, "Heads I **win**; tails I **win**!" He can't lose whether he lives or dies! That is the testimony of a Christian who is content in Christ.

Beware of Covetousness!

Jesus helps us understand this commandment through a personal encounter He had. The man is often called the Rich, Young Ruler. You can read about it in Mark 10:17–23:

> *As Jesus started on his way, a man ran up to him and fell on his knees before him. "Good teacher," he asked, "What must I do to inherit eternal life?" "Why do you call me good?" Jesus answered. "No one is good—except God alone. You know the commandments: 'Do not murder, do not commit adultery, do not steal, do not give false testimony, do not defraud, honor your father and mother.'" "Teacher," he declared, "all these I have kept since I was a boy." Jesus looked at him and loved him. "One thing you lack," he said. "Go, sell everything you have and give to the poor, and you will have treasure in heaven. Then come, follow me." At this the man's face fell. He want away sad, because he had great wealth. Jesus looked around and said to his disciples, "How hard it is for the rich to enter the kingdom of God!"*

This is one of the strangest conversations recorded in the New Testament. This young man asked the right question—but we have to scratch our heads at the reply of Jesus. Is the way to inherit eternal life to "keep the commandments?" That's not what Jesus told Nicodemus when he asked the same question. Jesus told Nicodemus (who kept all the commandments) "you must be born again." (John 3:7)

By now, you can hopefully recognize that Jesus quotes five of the six commandments that comprise the "second part" of the Decalogue —another term for the Ten Commandments. Every good Jew memorized the Ten Commandments, and they knew that the first tablet (Commandments one through four) dealt with a person's relationship with God—and that the second tablet (Commandments four through ten) dealt with human relationships. Jesus quotes these last six commandments—but He intentionally **OMITS** one! Did you notice which one Jesus left out? He names the last six commandments:

"Honor your father and mother, don't kill, don't commit adultery, don't steal and don't bear false witness." I believe that His omission was as obvious as if I attempted to quote the alphabet, "A B C _ E F ..." You would know immediately that I had left one letter out. I think everyone in that day noticed the ONE commandment that Jesus left out. The with a twinkle in His eye, Jesus said, "Those are the commandments you have to keep."

The wealthy young man replied, "I have kept every one of those commandments from the time I was young."

Jesus said, "Okay, there is **one thing** you lack." Did you notice the one commandment He intentionally left out? He didn't quote the tenth one—"You shall not **covet**." Why? Because Jesus had the ability to look into the heart of that rich, young ruler and know that gold was his god. The **one sin** that was separating him from God was **covetousness** or greed. Jesus said, "Okay, one more thing, go sell all you have, give it to the poor and follow me." The rich, young ruler considered Jesus. Then he considered all his riches, and the Bible says he went away sad. He made the wrong choice. Millions of Americans have made the same sad choice—they have opted for gold instead of God. Covetousness can keep you out of heaven.

This last commandment has to do with human **desire**, and it is an identical bookend to commandment one. Who is your God? Who is number one in your life? If it is anything or anyone other than Jesus Christ, you will never be satisfied.

The Eleventh Commandment

If America is going to survive into the 21st Century, we must reclaim these timeless moral standards that God has established. In August of 1999, the world was shocked to hear of the tragic earthquake in Turkey. Entire cities were destroyed and over 12,000 people lost their lives. In the aftermath of the killer quake, a disturbing story surfaced from that area.

It was discovered that in 1993, United Nations geologists and seismologists surveyed that part of Turkey. They discovered that a dangerous fault line ran through that area. One small village was especially at risk because it was actually built on the most dangerous part of the fault line. The Turkish government told the village leaders that they must move their village off the fault line. The officials even showed them a map with the village sitting on the fault line to prove their point and offered free land for the village to resettle.

However, the village leaders refused to leave. Instead, they bribed the mapmakers to "move" the fault line on the map so they wouldn't be forced to move. With the "new" map, the village was no longer on the fault line. Ten minutes after the killer quake struck, the village was gone, and nearly all the residents perished.

Our God has drawn some clear moral lines—fault lines to warn us of the danger of moral destruction. These lines are the Ten Commandments. However, America has been trying to "redraw" these moral lines to fit our modern culture—instead of moving to the safety of obedience. The result on our moral system will be similar to the tragic fate of the Turkish village—total collapse.

Before America can reinstate these basic standards of morality, our citizens (especially Christians) must regain a renewed understanding of them. The continued arguments over the Ten Commandments reveal once again that many of those on either side of the issue are woefully ignorant regarding the fundamental teaching of the commandments. It's my prayer that this practical understanding and application of God's commands has helped equip you as you seek to become more involved in the democratic process that makes our republic great. Equipped Christians who understand God's Word are the best ambassadors for the kingdom in a world where many misinterpret and misrepresent Scripture.

Above all, we must emphasize to others why God gave us these commands in the first place—simply because He loves us. He wants the best for us, and these guidelines reveal the loving heart of God for His people—something that, sadly, often gets lost amid heated arguments.

When asked what the greatest commandment was, Jesus replied, "'Love the Lord your God with all your heart and with all your soul and with all your mind.' This is the first and greatest commandment. And the second is like it: 'Love your neighbor as yourself.' All the Law and the Prophets hang on these two commandments" (Matt. 22:37–40).

When you truly love God, you won't violate the first four commandments. Likewise, when you sincerely love your neighbor, you won't have to worry about keeping the last six commandments. Will you pause right now and ask God to give you the strength to love Him more dearly? Will you ask Him to give you a deeper love for your neighbor? As God answers that prayer for you, His Ten Requirements will be a joy for you to follow, not a burden. Will you join me and hundreds of thousands of other Americans in reestablishing America's commitment to moral excellence? It CAN be done, one Christian and one citizen at a time.

Appendix

The Perfect Ten

In order to OBEY the Ten Commandments, you must MEMO-RIZE the Ten Commandments. Here is a simple poem by an unknown author that I have taught to children for many years. It can even help adults make a permanent mental file of God's Decalogue, the Ten Commandments:

> Number One, we've just begun—God should be first
>   in your life.
> Number Two's the idol rule—those graven images
>   aren't nice.
> Number Three, God's name should be—never
>   spoken in jest.
> Number Four, the Sabbath's for—our worship and
>   our rest.
> Number Five, we all should strive—to honor Father
>   and Mother.
> Number Six, don't get your kicks—from killing one
>   another.
> Number Seven, life is heaven—when you're true to
>   your mate.
> Number Eight, don't steal—and break this rule for
>   goodness sake!

Number Nine, don't be the kind—who goes around telling lies.

Number Ten, don't covet when—you see your neighbor's house—or wife.

That's the list—and God insists—we stay away from these sins.

That is why we memorize Commandments One through Ten!

What's Right with America?

Prior to the 1960s, the following facts and stories were staples in the American school textbook. Thanks to revisionist historians, however, these principles are slowly fading into our past. We must do our part to make sure future generations do not forget these foundational truths of our nation.

1. America was founded by God-fearing, Bible-believing people.

The original Mayflower Compact (1620) reads: "In the name of God, Amen, Having undertaken for the Glory of God and the advancement of the Christian faith do solemnly and mutually in the presence of God, covenant and combine ourselves together ..."

The 1643 Constitution of the New England Confederation clearly states: "Whereas we all come into these parts with one and the same end and aim—namely to advance the Kingdom of our Lord Jesus Christ and to enjoy the liberties of the Gospel in purity and peace."

2. America was protected and directed by God from the start.

George Washington claimed that were it not for DIVINE INTERVENTION, he would never have lived to see the Revolution. During the French and Indian War, Washington led troops into battle. In one battle, over 700 men were killed, and when the fighting stopped, Washington was the only soldier left on horseback. He looked down at his vest and put his finger into three bullet holes—but he didn't have a scratch on him. Fifteen years later, he returned to the site of the battle, and an old Indian chief, who was now an ally of Washington, said to him, "I wanted to meet the man that God had miraculously saved in that battle." The chief told Washington that he had instructed his braves to aim their muskets at him, knowing that if the leader were shot, the troops would retreat. All of the braves fired at Washington. Even the chief claimed that he had shot Washington 17 times—yet he remained unharmed.

3. America was founded by men who acknowledged God's supreme rule over humanity.

"We hold these truths to be self evident; that all men are created equal and are endowed by their CREATOR with certain inalienable rights, that among these are LIFE, LIBERTY, and the PURSUIT OF HAPPINESS—and that to secure these rights, governments are instituted among men...."

"We therefore the representatives of the United States of America, in general Congress, Assembled, appealing to the SUPREME JUDGE of the WORLD for the rectitude of our intentions ....."

"And for the support of this Declaration, with a firm reliance on the PROTECTION of DIVINE PROVIDENCE, we mutually pledge our Lives, our fortunes, and our sacred honor."

-from the Declaration of Independence, 1776-

Samuel Adams (the Father of the American Revolution) wrote four years before the Declaration of Independence: "The rights of the Colonists as Christians may be best understood by reading and studying the teachings of Jesus Christ, the head of the Christian Church, which are to be found clearly written and promulgated in the New Testament."

John Quincy Adams (whose father, John, signed the Declaration of Independence) wrote in 1821, "From the time of the Declaration of Independence, the American people were bound by the laws of God (and by the laws of the Gospel) which they all acknowledge as the rules of their conduct."

4. America's government is patterned after biblical principles.

There are different types of government—monarchy (rule by one); oligarchy (rule by a few); democracy (rule by the majority) and a republic (rule by law). For example, France has had 15 forms of government in its existence. Italy has had 48 different forms of government. In comparison, our system of government has remained unchanged for over 200 years.

America is a republic (which is why we state the Pledge of Allegiance) that elects its leaders through a democratic process. Where did our founding fathers get the idea for THREE BRANCHES of government (Executive, Legislative, and Judicial)? Regarding the answer to this question, Thomas Jefferson referred to Isaiah 33:22, "For the Lord is our JUDGE, our LAWGIVER, and our KING—it is He who will save us." Where did our government get the idea of protecting the church FROM the government and making the church tax-exempt? (It wasn't merely a revolutionary idea!) Ezra 7:24 states, "You are also to know that you have no authority to impose taxes , tribute, or duty on any of the priests, Levites, singers, servants or other workers at this house of God."

5. American law guarantees and protects our religious freedom.

In 1892, our highest court in the land stated, "Our laws and our institutions must necessarily be based on and must include the teachings of the redeemer of mankind. It's impossible for it to be otherwise. To this extent our civilization and our institutions are emphatically Christian."

In 1963, not even a century later, the Supreme Court ruled this school prayer unconstitutional: "To the Almighty God, we acknowledge our dependence on thee. We ask thy blessings upon us, our parents, our teachers, and our Country."

However, there is a higher Supreme Court than the US Supreme Court. Remember what the Declaration of Independence said about the SUPREME JUDGE OF THE WORLD? When the US Supreme Court says we cannot pray in public, it is time for humble, but conscientious CIVIL DISOBEDIENCE.

For instance, our law protects the church from government intervention and taxation. But what if a majority of people voted to disagree—would that change the law? No, because our First Amendment guarantees us freedom of religion. The First Amendment says, "Congress shall make no law respecting the establishment of religion, or prohibiting the free exercise thereof ..." The so-called "Wall of separation" between church and state was never intended to protect the government from Christian influence. It was designed to protect the church from governmental interference.

6. America Is Beautiful

In 1883, an English professor from Wellesley College near Boston, took a train trip west to see the sights of America. While in Colorado, she rode a horse-drawn wagon to the top of Pike's Peak , which rises 14,000 feet above sea level. That evening, when Katherine Lee Bates returned to her hotel room, she was so moved that she couldn't sleep. She got out a pen and paper and wrote:

> *Oh beautiful for spacious skies, For amber waves of grain,*
> *For purple mountain's majesty, above the fruited plain.*
> *America, America! God shed His grace on Thee,*
> *And crown thy good with brotherhood from sea to shining sea.*

Note her third verse:

> *O beautiful for heroes proved i liberating strife;*

Who more than self their country loved, and mercy
    more than life!
America, America! May God thy gold refine,
Till all success be nobleness, and every gain divine. [xi]

The tallest structure in Washington DC is the Washington Monument. Inscribed at the top are these words, "LET GOD BE PRAISED." America, it's time to lift up our eyes and say, "Let God be praised for our nation!"

Endnotes

i Ted Koppel, excerpted from his commencement speech to Duke University graduates, 1987.

ii Geiermann, Monsignor Peter. *A Doctrinal Catechism*, 1957 edition, p. 50.

iii Bonhoeffer, Dietrich. *Cost of Discipleship*, Touchstone Books, 1995.

iv Taken from an Associated Press article, *USA Today,* (July 26, 1996).

v Alighieri, Dante. From *The Divine Comedy*, (1265-1321).

vi Ten Boom, Corrie. *The Hiding Place*, Bantam, Reissue edition, 1984.

vii Hite, Shere. *The New Hite Report,* Hamlyn Publishers, 2000.

viii Patterson, James. Peter Kim, *The Day America Told the Truth: What People Really Believe about Everything That Really Matters*, Prentice Hall Trade, 1991.

xi Katharine Lee Bates, *America the Beautiful*, 1893.